PARENTING STYLES
UNLEASHED

A MODERN GUIDE
FOR IMPROVED FAMILY DYNAMICS

Paul Buckley, LMFT

Note: Parenting styles used throughout this book are generalizations. No single model, metaphor, or theoretical concept can contain all the various—and beautiful—permutations of any one person's life, let alone family dynamics. In the author's clinical experience, most people find these styles uncannily accurate and predictive of their family situations.

Front cover design by Lauren Swago
Book design by Claire Chamberlin
Illustrations by Sharon Davis
Author photo by Catching the Light Within / Scott Sater Photography

To the parents and children I have met over the course of three decades of helping families, this book is dedicated to you. Being invited into the sanctums of your private struggles has been an honor. The heartbreaking and heart-making stories enriched me and contributed to this book.

CONTENTS

FOREWORD

WHEN PAUL BUCKLEY ASKED ME to write a foreword to his book, Parenting Styles Unleashed, I felt aptly suited for his project—not because I was a great parent, perhaps, but just the opposite. With a bookshelf of over two dozen dog-eared parenting books, I was intimately familiar with parenting books. I loved them. They just didn't help.

My son, already eighteen, was past the age when therapists believed a parent had any significant influence. As I'd read in other books, developmentally, he was under the influence of his peers at this point.

Most importantly, his childhood had been marked with testosterone-fueled refusals and angry outbursts. High anxiety masked itself as "bad behavior." Diagnosed with ADHD at eight, he'd been on a merry-go-round of medications. Nothing seemed to improve his behavior or willingness to cooperate.

Within the first few chapters of Parenting Styles Unleashed, it became clear —quite quickly—the cracks in our parenting foundation. Chapter 1 identified parenting styles using canine avatars to illustrate the strengths and weaknesses of each "breed." Accepting there are multiple parenting styles eliminated my drive to discover the secret, single method to successful childrearing. It brought into the realm of possibility that opposites could parent effectively through understanding and modest adaptation.

I was clearly a BORDER COLLIE style who had been blaming our parenting problems squarely on my son's dad, a kind AFGHAN HOUND parent style. And by now, I had pretty much given up hope of any cooperation or even simply a smile from my son. He'd taken himself off all medication and refused any more therapy. Things seemed not destined to improve.

The chapter's Family Stress Test indicated our family was in the Red Zone. Our parenting had fallen into a self-perpetuating GOOD COP/BAD COP pattern. I was angry and resentful of always being the bad cop.

Possibly the most convincing argument I have for why this book worked when nothing else did, is that it helped me identify a problem therapists couldn't witness: the visible frustration I displayed in daily interactions with my son. My BORDER COLLIE parenting style and subconscious reactions to my son's underlying anxiety played an enormous part in perpetuating a tumultuous Frustration/Resistance Cycle.

Of all the therapy sessions and parenting books I'd read, it was this book that held the key to understanding my role in my son's behavior. It wasn't about setting clear-cut rules and doling out age-appropriate consequences, as many books had asserted. And most importantly, it worked whether or not a co-parent was on board!

Buckley describes the "brightening" one could expect in children as parents become emotionally attuned to the child. To my enormous surprise, as I made subtle changes in my emotional response, things began to improve. And as I changed, so did my son.

Within a few months, my son went from someone I fought and feared to a loving, laughing, and kind young man. Mr. Buckley noted that I had become a therapeutic influence in my son's life, helping him navigate his anxiety, frustration, and sadness. What an awesome gift to be able to give to your child.

I highly recommend this book's perspective and strategies on parenting and family dynamics.

—A grateful mom

PREFACE

NEVER HAS THE FAMILY BEEN MORE CHALLENGED. Social media dilutes parental influence, video games grab kids by the brain stem, identity issues proliferate beyond common understanding, and mind-warping substances swirl from gummies and vape pens. These are but a few of the factors that turn ratcheting tension in family life, stretching the fabric of emotional warmth between parents and children into a frazzle of sadness and anger. Among these diseases of social complexities, this book strives for something singular: enriching caregivers' connection, and therefore influence, with their children.

I have spent thirty years as a family therapist, trekking and tracking through the challenging wilderness of distressed families and disturbed children. Hundreds of home visits, stints at Level-III education settings, thousands of clinical hours, and an abundance of speaking engagements all provided panoramic and microcosmic views of the noble struggles and strivings of troubled families. No two were quite alike.

Over these years, experience and education tamed the wilderness. The landscape grew familiar. Patterns emerged. Marital discord lurched with the pain of confronting and retreating. Stressed children wrangled upset feelings by withdrawing anxiously or, externalizing aggressively, or merely numbing out in the black ink of Wi-Fi devices.

Attachment Theory and **Emotional Focused Therapy** explained and named these patterns, forming helpful trails for me as a therapist to guide others, especially caregivers, away from conflict and toward emotional connectedness.

This book then is written as a friendly yet serious guide for caregivers. The illustrations of familiar dog breeds, diagrams, Quick Quizzes, and stories of other families in therapy aim toward the heart of parents and caregivers, showing better paths for the noblest and most strenuous journey on earth—raising children.

INTRODUCTION

THE CHALLENGE

As a veteran family therapist, I know that, on any given day, some parents are barricading their child's bedroom door, enforcing a time-out while the child inside screams, pelting Legos against the wall. Others are sitting outside a principal's office, waiting to discuss their child's detention. A few rants ineffectually at the kids to shut off electronics and go outside while their partner is sequestered in the garage atop an overturned five-gallon pail, dragging on a forbidden cigarette. These scenarios hint at the stress, chaos, and often maddening challenges of family life.

One client, an officer at a detention center, admitted that she would rather stay late at work and face assaults and lockdowns than return home to the bedlam inflicted by her husband and two children. A dear friend of mine, who raised three children of her own and another twenty-three foster kids, has a placard in the kitchen proclaiming, "Raising children is like being pecked to death by chickens." In the aftermath of raising his boys, my brother wears a T-shirt, joking, "Of all the things lost while raising children, I miss my mind the most."

In a world of addictive electronic devices, corrosive social media, and rigorous school expectations, it's a marvel that any parent can raise a mentally healthy child and still retain their own sanity. Distress visits families in varying degrees but with clinically predictable results: uncertainty and insecurity can take over. Parents often become either dismissive or preoccupied with their child's upset feelings. Children begin resisting the simplest of requests and normal expectations. Couples polarize, isolate from, and judge one another. Family satisfaction falters as once-enjoyable routines crumble.

Even with these struggles, the mission of raising children can also be the most rewarding endeavor of one's life. This book offers understanding and effective strategies for a successful journey to family harmony.

"The first step to change is awareness."

NATHANIEL BRANDEN

The journey to awareness described herein begins with introducing the first of four basic parenting styles, each described using a canine avatar. The four furry friends describe four classic parenting styles, each with a distinct personality, unique enduring strength, and understandable vulnerability. The way these four avatars interact is key to understanding and solving problematic patterns and bringing joy back into your home.

In Chapter Two, you are invited to take the Family Stress Test to determine your family's Stress Zone. Are you in the good-to-go Green Zone, the more cautionary Yellow Zone, or the Stop, Look, and Listen Red Zone? More to discover ahead!

If you are in a co-parenting situation, you may already be acutely aware that parenting problems lead to partner problems. You will benefit by determining your partner's style to make it easier to comprehend why they may make seemingly ridiculous parenting decisions with such unhelpful results. Stressed couples are often greatly relieved to learn the parental differences that lead to maddening melees can improve and do so quite quickly! "It's a relief to know my husband hasn't been intentionally trying to drive me insane all these years," one client quipped. "But dammit, I'm not going to apologize for hiding his golf clubs."

There's enough hard work in family life. So let's proceed with a hopeful heart, believing the better part of discovery is joy, the greater part of humor is relief, and that this book will give you some of each.

WHY WE USE DOGS TO REPRESENT PARENTING STYLES

A while back, the office phone rang, and a woman said, "Hi, this is Talia, I attended one of your workshops a couple of years ago. I am a **BORDER COLLIE**, and my husband is an **AFGHAN HOUND**. We have two kids under twelve years old, one with ADHD, so you can imagine what we are going through."

"Sounds like you might be getting kind of burned out," I replied, "and your husband has probably checked out."

"We might be in the Red Zone," she continued, "I'm yapping at the kids all day long.

He's out in the garage doing God-knows-what, and I'm left being the 'bad cop.' I think we should see you before I boot him. I don't *want* to boot him out; I kind of like him."

I immediately understood what was happening in Talia's family because of our shared understanding of the terms BORDER COLLIE, AFGHAN HOUND, and The Red Zone. As a clinician, hearing they were a BORDER COLLIE/ AFGHAN HOUND couple in the Red Zone, I instantly knew what therapeutic direction would be most helpful.

Although Talia felt like booting her husband out, she hadn't done so yet. She had come to understand from my workshop that people have differing personalities and parenting styles. She came to accept that she and her husband were distinct breeds, both with their own unique parenting strengths and vulnerabilities. She now knew when personalities, tendencies, and traits clash, a path to harmony is possible. She no longer took her partner's parenting decisions personally. Talia understood that with awareness and a little guidance, they could parent their children more effectively and with better results.

With these four personality-packed dog breeds that convey complex information using playful and memorable avatars, like Talia, you will soon know yourself and your parenting partner (should you have one) as either a GOLDEN RETRIEVER, BORDER COLLIE, GERMAN SHEPHERD, or AFGHAN HOUND. With newfound awareness, you'll be on your way to better parenting and partnering strategies and methods.

Parenting partners who learn each other's personality tendencies will spark insight about why each might tug the parenting leash in a different direction.

THE MAP

The Dynamic Model of Marriage and Parenting (dmMAP), or, for our purposes, the Map, illustrates parent functioning with at-a-glance simplicity. The use of this tool provides a clear visual of where you—and your parenting partner (should you have one)— are on the Map.

When using a map, there are three essential questions to answer regarding family life as you journey forward:

Where are you?

Where do you want to be?

What is the best route to get there?

Developed from the sound and highly regarded field of Attachment and Relational Theory, the Map has been put into practice for over two decades in therapy sessions and workshops.

Like many caregivers before you, you can pinpoint your location on the Map and, having a visual anchor point, your journey to greater awareness begins, leading to better strategies—and ultimately—healthier family relationships. No more running in circles and chasing your tail!

With your heart as a compass and these tools as your map, you will soon learn to *unleash your parenting potential.*

Onward to **Section I: Awareness**. Discover your parenting style and take a Stress Test to determine your family's Stress Zone.

Quick Quiz

The author of the book wishes:

a. Parents learn about fascinating dog breeds

b. Readers suffer through another self-help book

c. Parents and caregivers deepen their connection and enhance their influence in the lives of children

SECTION I
AWARENESS

CHAPTER ONE

Discover Your Parenting Style

THE NURTURE SCALE

The first step to discovering your pooch parenting style is to find where you stand on the Nurture Scale, which is the horizontal dimension or, for the math-minded, the X-axis on the Map.

The Nurture Scale refers to how parents respond to their children's feelings. Some parents tend to provide more *comfort* to children; some tend to provide more *encouragement*. A classic example of that difference is the response to a child who has fallen off her bike and enters the house in tears with a bruised knee.

ENCOURAGE PARENT: "Whoops! Well, accidents happen. We'll ice that in a sec. The best thing to do now is get back on the bike. You can do it! Come on, I'll help you."

COMFORT PARENT: "Oh, honey, I am so sorry. That looks like it hurts. Maybe you should take a break. I'll get you an ice pack and a little snack."

Each response to the child's situation is reasonable and caring and yet, in essence, quite different. Looking at the Nurture Scale, which side best describes you?

THE NURTURE SCALE

ENCOURAGE   COMFORT

Encourage Parents engage most easily with a child's sense of curiosity and adventure. Their encouraging manner promotes exploration, adventure, and learning in a child's life.

Under stress, this action and future-oriented parent may become impatient or disengaged with family problems.

Comfort Parents attend to a child's feelings first and foremost. Uncomfortable with unresolved feelings they are motivated to soothe and fix the feelings of distressed children.

Under stress, this highly empathetic parent may seem pre-occupied with family problems.

Keep in mind that all parents comfort and encourage children according to the situation at hand. Placing yourself on the Nurture Scale is analogous to identifying yourself as right or left-handed. You certainly *can* do things with both hands, but you have a tendency to use your dominant hand. Used most often, the dominant hand becomes habituated and more proficient. Likewise, with nurturing, parents typically apply their dominant style most often while parenting.

At this point, you may have already decided which side of the Nurture Scale describes you best. But for those still uncertain, the following examples might help. Here's an example of each style responding to an upset fourth grader:

First: a look at the **COMFORT** Parent:

COMFORT PARENT: "Oh, my goodness, what happened? Why are you upset?"

CHILD: "I failed my math quiz. Now everyone thinks I'm stupid."

COMFORT PARENT: "Oh, honey, I'm sure no one thinks that. Everyone likes you. Why don't we have a snack and go to the park for a while?

CHILD: "I'm tired of everybody telling me what to do. I hate this stupid family!"

COMFORT PARENT: "Honey, I know you don't mean that. We all love you. Looks like you're just having a bad day."

Child stomps upstairs, and slams his bedroom door shut.

COMFORT PARENT (following child upstairs): "Honey, we should talk."

Next: the **ENCOURAGE** Parent

ENCOURAGE PARENT: "You look like you had a bad day. What's wrong?"

CHILD: "I failed my math quiz. Now everyone thinks I'm stupid."

ENCOURAGE PARENT: "Oh, I doubt that. You'll show them by getting an 'A' next time. This time, try doing more homework and less video games."

CHILD: "Everybody's telling me what to do. I hate this stupid family!"

ENCOURAGE PARENT: "Lower your voice, please, I'm trying to help."

Child stomps upstairs, and slams his bedroom door shut.

ENCOURAGE PARENT: "Sorry you're having such a bad day. If you want to come downstairs after you've calmed down, I'll be in the kitchen."

Notice how each parent conveys a different emotional tone to an upset child? Parents on the Comfort side of the scale typically attend to their children until problems are resolved. "Kids need us to be there" is the tagline of the Comfort Parent. And for that reason, upset children seek them out for solace.

Parents on the Encourage side of the scale typically respond less deeply to upset feelings, instead preferring to course correct or move on to something else entirely. The tagline of the Encourage Parent is, "Let's not dwell on it."

As mentioned, your preference is like being right or left-handed. Choosing your nurture style simply means you are more comfortable with one approach over the other, though capable of both!

Okay, it's time to choose. Which side of the Nurture Scale do you prefer: ENCOURAGE or COMFORT?

Put the doggie treat on the side of the scale that best describes you!

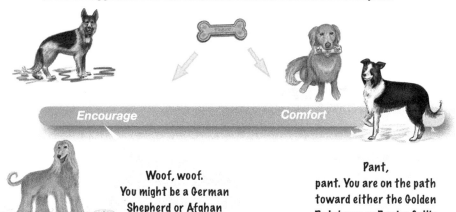

Encourage

Comfort

Woof, woof.
You might be a German
Shepherd or Afghan
Hound!

Pant,
pant. You are on the path
toward either the Golden
Retriever or Border Collie
Style.

Quick Quiz

Upset children tend to first seek out ...

a. The ENCOURAGE parent

b. The COMFORT parent

c. The nice lady with the cat next door

d. Gaming websites

THE STRUCTURE SCALE

The next step determines where you stand on the Structure Scale. This is the vertical dimension, or for the math-minded, the Y axis on the Map.

This scale describes how parents establish a structure for their children or, simply put, how parents form and enforce rules and routines.

From getting to the bus on time and completing homework to playing kindly with others and preparing for bedtime, family structure guides children as they master *The Three Rs: Rules, Respect, and Responsibilities*. Other terms for structure include *discipline, child management, and consequences*. But in this book, we use the term *family structure*.

When implementing a family structure, some parents are FLEXIBLE, some more FIRM. Which are you? Let's find out!

FLEXIBLE PARENTS have a relaxed manner when implementing The 3Rs. Rules and routines flex according to the situations and conditions at hand. Household expectations bend in consideration of the many factors that influence family life. For example, maybe it's okay to allow a school night sleepover of a special friend for a child who has been struggling with friendships. Of course, rules are important, but without considerations for individual circumstances, what do you have? A household, *too confining and dispiriting,* believes this parent!

Under stress, this FLEXIBLE parenting style may become inconsistent or even chaotic. More about this as we go.

FIRM PARENTS have a steadfast manner while administering The 3Rs of family life. Consistency and consequences are faithfully applied to family matters. Developing a child's character is a critical matter worthy of a parent's firm presence, whether a child is happy about the consequences or not. Sure, kindness and patience are important, but without a clear and enforced family policy, what do you have? *Chaos* thinks this parent!

Under stress, this principal-based parenting style may become authoritarian and controlling. More about this as we go.

Like the previously discussed Nurture Scale's "comfort and encourage" continuum, all parents can be both FLEXIBLE or FIRM, but Personality Theory[1] indicates that people have an inclination toward one side of the continuum or the other. Moreover, what is used most often becomes modus operandi, or habit, regarding family structure.

The following example illustrates the difference between FLEXIBLE & FIRM parents.

First a look at the FLEXIBLE Parent:

CHILD: "I know it's homework time, but all my friends are playing soccer at the park. Can I go? Please, can I go?"

FLEXIBLE PARENT: "Sounds like fun. Is your homework done?"

CHILD: "No, but I can do it later, I promise. Just this once? The whole neighborhood is there!"

---

[1] The Big Five Personality Traits: Agreeableness, Conscientiousness, Neuroticism, Openness to experience, Extroversion

FLEXIBLE PARENT: "Your grades have not been the best . . ."

CHILD (BEGINS TO CRY): "You have to let me go! I already told them I would play!"

FLEXIBLE PARENT: "Well, okay. You can go this time, but you have to promise to finish all your homework tonight. I mean it!

CHILD: "Okay, I promise!! Thanks!"

Next, the FIRM Parent:

CHILD: "I know it's homework time, but all my friends are playing soccer tonight at the park. Can I go? Please, can I go?"

FIRM PARENT: "You know the rules. Is your homework done?"

CHILD: "No, but I can do it later, I promise. Just this once? The whole neighborhood is there!"

FIRM PARENT: "If you get busy right now, you will be done in time to play, at least for a while."

CHILD (BEGINS TO CRY): "But they already started! Why can't I just go now?

FIRM PARENT: "Sorry, if you had spent this time working on your homework, you'd be on your way to completing your work. You know the rule; homework first.

The FLEXIBLE Parent considers situational complexities, such as the child's feelings, neighborhood involvement, and the promise to complete work later. With the FLEXIBLE Parent, the child might play soccer and complete their homework as promised, or perhaps whine and delay some more. The FIRM Parent provides clear expectations and administers the virtue of "work before play." Regarding important matters, duty and self-discipline come before relaxation and entertainment. With the FIRM Parent, the child may refuse to do their homework or, in seeing their parent's resolve, get busy and complete their work in order to play soccer.

The homework outcomes are impossible to predict, but clearly, each parent falls on a different side of the FIRM & FLEXIBLE scale.

Okay, once again, drop your doggie treat on the Map. Remember, being FIRM does not mean you don't flex now and then, and vice versa. It simply means you are inclined one way over the other.

Put the doggie treat on the side of the Structure Scale that best describes you.

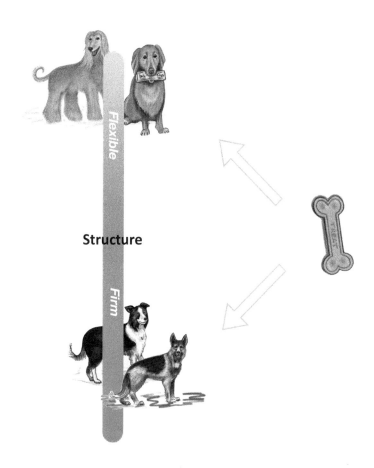

Combine the Nurture and Structure Scales, as shown below, to sniff out the quadrant best represents YOU:

Flexible

Afghan Hound Style:
Easy-going yet prone to becoming emotionally checked out.

Golden Retriever Style:
Compassionate yet prone to becoming emotionally overwhelmed.

Encourage

Comfort

German Shepherd Style: Principled yet prone to becoming emotionally insensitive.

Border Collie Style:
Attentive yet, during stressful times, prone to micromanaging others.

Firm

Well done! The avatar you have chosen will be your companion dog along your adventurous journey of insight and harmony. You now identify with one of four splendid dog breeds: The compassionate **GOLDEN RETRIEVER** the attentive **BORDER COLLIE**, the principled **GERMAN SHEPHERD**, or the easygoing **AFGHAN HOUND**.

CHAPTER TWO

The Family Stress Test

IN THIS CHAPTER, we'll determine where you and your family are on the Map in terms of family dynamics. Are you in the good-to-go Green Zone, the cautionary Yellow Zone, or (WOOF!) the hazardous Red Zone?

Establishing where you are in the Stress Zones is critical to your journey. A struggling child equals a worried parent. Whether the child is whining about going to school, avoiding homework, crying about lack of friends, fighting with siblings, or arguing about the littlest things, caregivers struggle for answers.

Parents wonder, 'Is this just a stage they'll grow out of ?' 'Should we apply tough love and hard consequences, or just wait it out?' 'Are things getting worse?' To help answer these questions and gain perspective about the degree of discord your family is experiencing, let's determine which Zone best describes where you are on the Map: Red, Green, or Yellow.

The MAP shows three colored rings or zones. These colors can be interpreted as a stop light:

GREEN = GO

YELLOW = CAUTION

RED = STOP, LOOK AND LISTEN

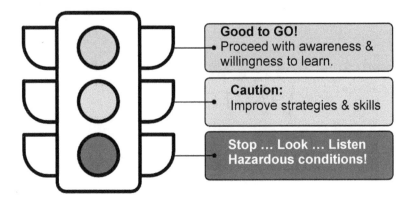

Good to GO!
Proceed with awareness & willingness to learn.

Caution:
Improve strategies & skills

Stop ... Look ... Listen
Hazardous conditions!

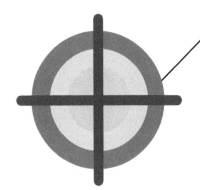

These colors correspond to the concentric color rings on the MAP

Trot ahead to explore which Stress Zone best describe your family situation.

Stress Test: PART ONE

Read the following paragraphs and pick the number on the scale that best describes your family situation, with 1 being the best ever and 9 being two digits away from a 911 call.

GREEN ZONE FUNCTIONING: Our family knows how to have fun with one another! There are times of conflict and misunderstandings, but these times are handled with apologies and heart to heart conversations.

In general, children take responsibility for homework, chores, and helping out around the house. Morning and bedtime routines are fairly smooth and peaceful. Sibling relationships are generally kind. Occasionally there's arguing and yelling, but in general, tempers settle fairly quickly. Media use is managed responsibly.

My partner and I have occasional parenting disagreements although we find ways of supporting each other. My work and social life are not impeded by worry about family distress.

YELLOW ZONE FUNCTIONING: Our family enjoys each other but too often something goes wrong, which leads to hurt feelings. These feelings create resentment that boils over at times. Family responsibilities often turn into complaint and anger. Morning and bedtime routines are often stressful.

Sibling conflict occurs too often. Children fall into stereotypic roles like the "good kid," the "problem child," "my little helper," etc. Media use is a problem.

Childrearing decisions with my partner are difficult. Because of this, we often don't work as a team. Work and social life are being affected by worrying about home life.

RED ZONE FUNCTIONING: Our family struggles to enjoy each other. Family members carry a chronic chip on their shoulder from so many disappointments.

Basic routines, such as bedtime and homework completion are rarely accomplished without a battle of wills. Sibling relationships strain with conflict and resentments. Each child seems locked into certain roles. Media use is a real problem.

Making decisions with my partner is nearly impossible. One, or both of us, seems to have just given up. My work and social life are impacted, in part because of 'fight fatigue' and because I'm afraid of what I'll come home to.

PART ONE SCORE: _____

Stress Test Part 2

Circle the number that best describes your parenting/family situation, then add them up for a total score. *(Score "0" if the question is not applicable)*

1) In our family I (we) end up using loud and frustrated voices in order to get things done.

      1 —   Hardly ever
      2 —   A few times a week
      3 —   On a daily basis

2) The amount of time having fun in our family seems to be shrinking. So much time is spent arguing or avoiding conflict.

      1 —   False
      2 —   True

3) My children intentionally make me angry.

      1 —   Seldomly
      2 —   A few times a week
      3 —   Nearly daily

4) Going to work (or just leaving the house) is a relief from stressful family life.

      1 — Not really
      2 — Sometimes
      3 — Often

5.) My partner and I discuss parenting issues and agree on most matters.

      1 — Often
      2 — Sometimes
      3 — Almost never

6) Family routines, such as morning and bedtimes …

      1 — are generally peaceful and smooth
      2 — at times cause problems
      3 — often results in frustration and complaint
      4 — has been a problem for over a 6 months

7) My partner undermines my parenting efforts.

      1 — Seldom
      2 — Sometimes
      3 — Often

8) My children resist normal expectations with anger, blame, and refusals.

      1 — Occasionally
      2 — Regularly
      3 — Often

9) When significant conflicts occur between family members, they are addressed and settled in a timely manner.

      1 — Nearly always
      2 — Sometimes
      3 — Seldom

10) Unsettled resentments exist between me and my parenting partner.
        1 — Not really
        2 — Sometimes
        3 — Often

11) To keep the peace I find myself ignoring family problems.
        1 — Not really
        2 — Sometimes
        3 — Often

12) My child(ren) seem defensive, sullen, or angry much of the time.
        1 — Not really
        2 — Sometimes
        3 — Often

13) Family issues negatively my child(ren) at school and other settings.
        1 — Not really
        3 — Sometimes
        4 — Often

14) My child(ren) are difficult at home AND at other people's homes.
        1 — Not really
        3 — Sometimes
        4 — Often

15) My worry about family dynamics caused me sleep loss, worry, and stress.
        1 — Not really
        3 — Sometimes
        4 — Often

SCORING

_____ **+** _____ **=** _____
(PART 1 SCORE)   (PART 2 SCORE).   (FINAL SCORE)

WHAT YOUR SCORE MEANS

0 TO 11: GREEN ZONE

Yours is a resilient family where subtle parenting changes generate progress quite quickly. Naturally, there are moments of frustration for your family, but they have not yet formed into entrenched, bad habits. Learning new parenting strategies is always helpful.

12 TO 17: YELLOW ZONE

Repeating cycles of parental frustration and child resistance are forming unhealthy habits. Left unchecked, family distress will remain the same, or worsen. Slow down, address recurring problems, and employ new strategies. Proceed with CAUTION.

18 AND UP: RED ZONE

Conditions are hazardous. Entrenched problems are causing recurring conflict and general unhappiness resulting in a distressed family environment. It's time to change course using improved parenting and interpersonal practices. STOP, look, and listen.

CONGRATULATIONS CAREGIVER! By discovering your parenting avatar and the Stress Zone that best describes your family situation, you have started down the Awareness path toward understanding your parenting style, your co-parent, and ultimately, a happier family life. Well done! Now, let's march forward to a deeper understanding of your parenting style. In the chapters to follow, veils of confusion will gradually lift, shedding light on your parenting and co-parenting dynamics.

Jump now to the chapter describing your parenting avatar. After reading about your parenting style, next read about the traits of your parenting partner's breed, should you have one. The chapter formats for each dog breed are similar: highlighting Parenting Strengths in Action and how things go sideways in the turbulent Yellow and Zones.

Quick Quiz

The Family Stress Test is meant to...

a. Blame your children for the utter madness of family life.

b. Blame your partner for the utter madness of family life.

c. Measure distress in order to create awareness and strategic thinking.

CHAPTER THREE

The Golden Retriever Parenting Style

"A spoonful of sugar helps
the medicine go down."

MARY POPPINS

IF YOU HAVE IDENTIFIED YOURSELF as a GOLDEN RETRIEVER parent, this chapter is for you. The GOLDEN RETRIEVER'S genealogy reaches back to the 1800s, rendering a spirited canine eager to fetch and respond. This kindly breed—and parenting style—generates homes filled with kindness and love. How does your canine avatar translate to the furless parenting world?

LET'S TAKE A LOOK!

AT THEIR BEST, this parent patiently and compassionately provides emotional warmth and kindness to others and gracefully guides and cajoles children through daily routines and responsibilities.

AT THEIR WORST, this parent becomes overwhelmed and preoccupied with the upset feelings of others; in a distressed household, vacillates between complaining and a silent martyr.

DOMINANT BELIEFS: Love will conquer all. Be nice to others, and they will be nice in return.

LOVES to love and be loved.

CO-PARENTING: sniffs out principled GERMAN SHEPHERDS or easygoing AFGHAN HOUNDS.

— — — — — — — — — — — — —

THE GENTLE GOLDEN RETRIEVER parent style nurtures the hearts and minds of children, but the heart comes first. Therefore their dog tags reads:

PARENTING STRENGTHS IN ACTION

The **GOLDEN RETRIEVER** parent deserves an appreciative hug. They provide so much and ask for so little! Children swarm to the household of the GR parent. Kind words, tasty snacks, and gentle admonishments are dispensed through the parent's welcoming eyes and dulcet tones. And what is their reward for these parenting efforts? Simply, that joy and peace flourishes within the home, and their own children go to bed, giving toothpaste-flavored kisses. The caring GR heart fosters and fuels a child's well-being and growth.

As the psychology field, research, and experience repeatedly show, emotionally "tuned-in" caregivers provide an essential precondition for optimal child development. Give that dog a bone!

In the workplace, this compassionate breed is often at home in the fields of education, social work, and medicine. They pursue and excel in careers where relationships, nurturing, and social contact matter.

LOCATION ON THE MAP

Let's take a minute to appreciate the supple psyche of the **GOLDEN RETRIEVER** parenting style. The GR is found on the quadrant on the Map between **COMFORT & FLEXIBLE**.

First, take an in-depth look at the **GOLDEN RETRIEVER** on the Nurture Scale.

NURTURE SCALE = How this parent responds to a child's feelings. The GR is most at home on the COMFORT end of the Nurture Scale. Comforting generates emotional connectedness, especially for children experiencing upset feelings. This connectedness is restorative in nature, meaning it is...*capable of renewing health and strength.* The soothing emotional tones slow a child's mind to a "here and now" embrace. This GR parent and child talk and feel their way through problems and dilemmas. This shared intimacy helps the child process their strong emotions, fosters deep understanding, and paves the way for the child to learn and develop.

Toddler falls down, go boom? Best to hug and hold him until he's ready to toddle again. Teen didn't make the varsity team? Best to let her cry and talk about her disappointment within the secure arms of an understanding parent. Within this mystic brew of closeness and compassion, a child acquires a richer understanding of the world and what to do next, whether it means rededication to more practice or seeking out a new interest.

Let's take a look at the **GOLDEN RETRIEVER** parenting style on the Structure Scale. Structure Scale = refers to the preferred manner of discipline and teaching The 3Rs (Rules, Respect, and Responsibilities). The GR leans toward the FLEXIBLE end of the Structure Scale.

The GR administers discipline (The 3Rs) by persuading and adjusting to the situation at hand. Rule and order are important, the GR believes, but so are feelings. Instilling the lessons and habits of life becomes a subtle dance between parent and child, a waltz of coaxing and inducing. Yes, it's an interactive complexity requiring both patience and grace.

The GR's combined attributes—COMFORT & FLEXIBLE— cajole and console children, who enjoy being in an orb of affection even though they may feel smothered at times.

Keep in mind, this COMFORT & FLEXIBLE tendency falls on a continuum. The GR parent can administer household rules, and will certainly encourage them, but there will be slight bias toward their natural style.

An example of a GR parent handling a child who is running late for school in the morning:

THE GOLDEN RETRIEVER, THE CHILD, AND THE SHOE

CHILD (running through the house): "I can't find my other shoe, and the bus is coming. Help me find my shoe!"

GR: "Oh no. Where did you put them last?" (GR begins to look for the shoe with the child.)

CHILD: "I don't know! Why didn't you wake me up on time?"

GR: "I'm sorry honey, but calm down, okay? I'm trying to help you. You know this happens all the time. Maybe we should have a place for the shoes?"

CHILD: "MOM! The bus is here!"

GR: "Well, we'll look until we find it. I'll make time to drive you to school this time. But from now on, make sure you know where both shoes are, please."

WHAT'S GOING ON IN THIS EXAMPLE?

The child is upset about the shoe and looks outside herself for a solution. The kind and empathetic GR sees their distress and the GR's first instinct is to soothe the child's pain. The GR offers assistance to help solve the child's problem with support and warmth in an attempt to assure the child that everything will be okay. When the child blames the parent (like all children sometimes do), the GR even apologizes to calm the waters. The hope is within these calmer waters, progress will be made, and lessons will be learned.

ATTACHMENT THEORY AND THE GOLDEN RETRIEVER PARENT

Attachment Theory is the psychological school of thought that shows how children flourish and develop through attuned and connected attachment with their caregivers.

Children benefit from caregivers who:

1) *Encourage* them to explore

2) *Support* them while they *persevere* through roadblocks in their exploration

3) *Comfort* them in order they may *recover* from fatigue, upset feelings, and setbacks

Congrats, GOLDEN RETRIEVER! You SUPPORT children as they persevere, and COMFORT them as they recover from their efforts!

As you might guess, the GR parent is a natural at comforting but may be a bit awkward or disinclined in promoting adventures and activities that involve risk.

Here's an example of a Golden Retriever parent in action:

While playing basketball with the neighbor kids, young Henry was pushed and fell. He enters the house, angry and sad.

GR PARENT: "Oh goodness, what happened? Here, let's put a cool washcloth on that. I bet that hurts."

HENRY: "It hurts a LOT. That stupid Max pushed me. He never plays fair."

GR: "Oh dear, let's put a bandage on it, too. So Max pushed you, huh?"

HENRY: "He's a bully, and now all the kids think I'm weak. No one will play with me ever again because I always get hurt and cry!" (Henry starts to cry in deep sobs.)

GR: "Well, I'm proud of you for feeling such big feelings and telling me all this. It takes special courage to do this—more courage than it takes to push a friend."

HENRY: "I think I'll tell the guys I'm going to take a break and shoot baskets some other time."

GR: "Sounds good to me. I bet we could find something interesting to do in the house."

HENRY: "Yeah, okay."

Henry and his compassionate GR parent are attuned and connected to each other, allowing Henry to solve his problem while feeling securely attached to his mother. This gentle exchange has also done something else. Henry feels understood and guided by his parent's empathy. With his attuned parent, Henry brightens into a more cooperative stance that helps him emotionally self-regulate. This gives him practice for other conflicts that will come his way.

Support and comfort...well done, GR! As far as encouraging Henry to get back in the game, well, that's not this dog's best trick. At least not yet...

THE GOLDEN RETRIEVER'S PREFERRED METHOD OF GUIDING CHILDREN: PERSUASION

Each of our four canine avatars has its own signature strategy of getting children to do what is expected of them. All parents use a variety of methods to guide and motivate children, but each parent pooch has their own distinct method, especially when stressed. Here are the four primary strategies: the principled GERMAN SHEPHERD enforces, the easygoing Afghan finesses, the attentive BORDER COLLIE compels. And what of the compassionate GOLDEN RETRIEVER? This parenting style's favored method is to persuade.

> **per·sua·sion** /pər'swāZHən/ *noun*: the action or fact of persuading someone or of being persuaded to do or believe something.

The three stages of *persuasion*:

1.*Reminding* about the situation at hand

2.*Coaxing* using explanations and tone of voice

3.*Warning* about consequences and outcome

Reminding is the GR's tool for prompting a child to get something done. This implies the child forgot, but is willing to be helpful.

Coaxing addresses the problem of a child's lack of motivation to be immediately cooperative. The GR employs a subtle shift in tone of voice with explanations about what needs to get done and how.

Warning suggests negative consequences will occur, thereby amplifying the child's fear-based motivation.

In each stage, the GR attempts to persuade underlying motivation systems in the child in order to accomplish a goal.

Here's an example of a Golden Retriever parent in action at Funland Amusement Park:

GR (reminding): "Okay, Jocelyn, I'll meet you right here at three o'clock. Here's fifty dollars. Have fun, Sweetie."

Forty minutes later, Jocelyn returns with a poster sticking out of her backpack, a plush toy clipped to her belt loop, and sipping a chocolate milkshake.

JOCELYN: "Wow, everything is so expensive here! Can I have some more money? Maddie's dad gave her forty dollars to spend, and we want to ride the roller coaster."

GR (coaxing): "Honey, I need you to be more careful of how much you're spending. You don't need to buy all that junk. Here's ten more dollars, but that's all."

Twenty minutes later, Jocelyn returns.

JOCELYN: "Geez, this place is a rip off! Could you please give me just ten more dollars so Maddie and I can do one more ride? You can take it out of my allowance."

GR (warning): "Okay, honey, but when it comes out of your allowance I don't want to hear any complaining later. Next time, you'll have to plan your spending better. And I'm serious."

This method appeals to the cooperative nature of children, as the parent verbally modulates appeals up or down in order to get things done. As a turbo-boost, the parent may add some volume or change their tone of voice. As is often the case, this parent may even layer on a little guilt (a GR signature method).

Childrearing is a nuanced endeavor for the big-hearted GR caregiver. With keen intuition, GR's peer deeply into a child's heart and ask important questions. How will an imposed consequence affect the child's well-being? How upset will the child become? Is the real issue behind a child's misbehavior that Mom and Dad work too much, or a younger sibling who succeeds so easily? The list is endless. In short, this parent can make fairly simple decisions quite complicated.

DIFFICULTIES FOR THE GOLDEN RETRIEVER PARENT

Being the emotional first responder is heavy lifting for any parent, and even more so when you add a host of career demands, children's academic and extracurricular activities, and caring for elderly parents. When extra layers of complications burden families, a child often acquires an ache for their caregivers, and especially for the GR parent who effuses love to children who are thirsty for just such a drink. This parent may falter under the weight of multiple burdens.

Additionally, GR's often become the target of a child's projected anger and blame, and must endure dramatic outbursts. This happens, as you may intuitively know, because the more emotionally available—and therefore safe—the more likely this caregiver becomes a target. If the child's problems with the heart are fairly normal, as in the Green Zone, the GR might sort it out if they can avoid taking things too personally, becoming preoccupied, or being overwhelmed. This parenting style, so filled with understanding and compassion, can become worn and frayed at the edges. Family stress can nudge the GR into the Yellow and Red Zones on the Map, from comforting to overwhelmed, from flexible to chaotic.

We'll talk more about this soon.

CO-PARENTING WITH A GOLDEN RETRIEVER PARENT

The GR is the expert on the child's feelings—especially sad or hurt feelings. The GR listens and attends to the feelings of upset children.

On the other side of this formulation, the co-parenting **AFGHAN HOUND** or **GERMAN SHEPHERD** provides an activating presence toward childhood purpose and play.

A few predictable patterns emerge. Upset children first seek out the GR parent for comfort, and soon learn to tap them to solve their problems. The GR loves to love, and be loved, but not to the point of exhaustion.

It's important for the GOLDEN RETRIEVER'S partner to lean into the childrearing process to provide relief to the GOLDEN RETRIEVER parent who fatigues from the persisting emotional demands of others.

THE GOLDEN RETRIEVER PARENTS IN THE TURBULENT YELLOW AND RED ZONES

What could possibly go wrong for the kindly GR, so willing to attend and attune to the feelings of others? As you might guess, a *lot* can go wrong, and it does so with tension headaches, and high drama. Think of all the demands and complexities of modernity: transitions to and from school, academic expectations, extracurricular activities, managing electronic devices, social media dramas, gender fluidity...and who knows what else! Then, add the possibility of parenting as a single parent or within a blended family, and the compassion of the GR is surely tested and depleted.

If stranded in the stormy Yellow Zone for too long, the stressed **GOLDEN RETRIEVER** caregiver morphs from their kindly self to becoming preoccupied with children's upset feelings. Inconsistency and shifting moods infiltrate the parent's psyche. Unresolved issues begin to take on a twisted life of their own.

In the Red Zone, those unresolved issues exceed the GR's capacity to self-manage. Drama and chaos reign. Children scream and cry, partners argue and point fingers, and sadness seeps in from all sides.

THE FRUSTRATION/RESISTANCE CYCLE

In a classic physics experiment, striking one tuning fork will cause a neighboring tuning fork to resonate at the same frequency. Frustration/Resistance is the family dynamic where a parent's visible frustration activates a child's resistance like two tuning forks resonating with each other. To understand its powerful influence over the emotions within the family, it deserves further exploration.

Intuitively, adults know a smile and rolling a ball toward a toddler will produce a smile and a ball rolled back. A parent's pleasant demeanor induces pleasant feelings in children. This cultivates a bloom of positive potential as children imitate, mimic, and cooperate with caregivers.

Less intuitive for caregivers is how an unpleasant parental interaction produces uncomfortable feelings in children. This spins a web of resistance toward their caregivers. When a parent uses an annoyed or irritable tone to send their child to bed, the child will undoubtedly whine and resist.

*This hard-wired, psychosocial phenomenon
exists within all social animals as they
imitate, mimic, and attune to each other in
a responsive, reflexive manner.*

Frustration is the uncomfortable feeling that occurs when intentions are thwarted and expectations aren't met. Each day, parents have numerous intentions and expectations. They intend to go to work, make nutritional meals, and raise good children. And from dawn to dusk, they expect their kids to get up, get dressed, get out the door, do homework, and go to bed. When caregivers display frustration, the inevitable result is a child's resistance.

On a good day, a child may rise above their natural inclination to resist the demands of a frustrated adult and get ready before the bus comes. The parent may have banked enough goodwill to not trigger resistance or, up to this point, the child has not had to endure multiple frustrations.

On a bad day, tolerance levels are depleted, and the child succumbs to the desire to resist— subconsciously landing a counterpunch by stalling or arguing— and misses the bus.

In the Yellow and Red Zones, parental frustration and child resistance feed each other; spinning like a dog chasing its tail...and getting nowhere. This parent trap is called the Frustration/Resistance Cycle.

These troubled zones generate hungry hearts and hurt feelings. Flooding the family with upset feelings overwhelms this sympathetic breed. The GR sinks into a defeated world of emotional confusion. And when problems persist, their parenting strength of emotional connectedness deteriorates.

Comforting morphs into what Attachment Theory describes as *preoccupation* or *enmeshment*. The embattled GR begins to have difficulty emotionally separating themselves from their children. Perspective blurs and everything feels personal. Family structure deteriorates from flexible to inconsistent and erratic. Within this painful place, a parent desperate for a modicum of control often vacillates between coddling to scolding kids, from feeling like a victim to manipulating kids by inducing guilt. Doggone it, this is a tough place to be!

Let's take a look at the Frustration/Resistance Cycle in action by peeking into the life of a Yellow Zone GOLDEN RETRIEVER parent looking for a little cooperation from a child:

> Transitioning from one activity to another requires emotional effort, also known as motivation. Transitioning from a passive stance to an active stance, such as cooperating with a parent, requires effort and higher-order functioning. Parents are more successful activating children when using pleasant tones of acceptance and gentle guidance. This calm space and time allows room for the child to transition.

STRESSED GR: "I thought I told you to pick up the family room. I asked you two hours ago! How many times do I have to ask you to do one simple chore around here?"

SERENA: "Why now? Nobody's coming over, are they?"

STRESSED GR: "That doesn't matter. It's a mess! I've asked you a thousand times: Pick-up-the-family-room, period!! I am tired of being the only one who cleans around here. Maybe being grounded for a couple weeks might help. No TV, no computer, no friends over. I'm sick and tired of this!"

SERENA: "All you do is yell and nag at me. All my friends have nice parents, but you always yell at me! Why do I have to be the one to pick up the family room? I'm not the only one who hangs out there!"

STRESSED GR: "Forget it. Never mind that I drove you to the mall. I'll pick it up myself! I do everything around here anyway."

In the above example, the child doesn't *intend* to be bratty, nor does the parent *intend* to nag. Both are stuck in a cycle of parental frustration and child resistance. Parent and child are like tuning forks resonating with each other, but attuned in *emotional distress*.

When this happens, the child is less likely to be able to face the challenge of cleaning the room, which includes transitioning from what the child *was* doing to cleaning up.

When frustration and resistance continue, it spreads and multiplies. Children begin to realize dramatic protests, relentless complaining, and persistent avoidance work, so they do more of it. Sooner or later, the child becomes intuitively aware of exactly what it will take for the parent to give in. Each mirrors the other in a twisting, downward spiral of irritated demands and angry protests.

In the Green Zone, this type of interaction occurs occasionally; in the Yellow Zone, regularly; and in the Red Zone, all too frequently. When this prickly pattern begins to grow, it's time to reach for help.

CHILDREN OF THE STRESSED GOLDEN RETRIEVER PARENT

When stressed, the GR parent becomes dramatic. Overwhelmed by taking on too much, the GR resorts to nagging, yelling, threatening, or using guilt to control the child. Children respond in kind and eventually wear down these peace-loving parents. By fifth grade, most children—through trial and error, or intuition—have discovered which approach works best and with which parent. This, by the way, is evidence of good emotional intelligence.

Children of a stressed GR caregiver eventually learn the use of high drama has a good chance of getting them off the hook. A highly upset child may induce a compassionate softening on the part of the GR, who worries they have overwhelmed the child's capacity. The tenderhearted GR might then reduce or remove the expectation on the child. The child learns exactly how long and how hard to cry to either get what they want or completely derail the caregiver.

Unfortunately, there are dark implications for children if families operate in the troubled Yellow and Red Zones for too long. Sure, children may avoid their responsibilities by overwhelming a parent now and then. But in the long run, is this what they really need? Of course not. Parental disapproval and the child's failure to accomplish The 3Rs (Rules, Respect, and Responsibility), diminishes the child's self-esteem and capacity to handle the myriad of childhood tasks.

Of particular concern is the **GOLDEN RETRIEVER** parent becoming so distressed and enmeshed in family matters that their parenting capacities become stretched and exceeded. The GR's compassion dwindles into a fervent list of grievances or somber surrender.

Under this chaotic cloud, a child loses their connection to a calm and caring adult. The loss is twofold. First, there is a generalized disruption of emotional stability. Second, the child loses the ability to process emotions. When children are unable to fully share their intense feelings of frustration and anger, or their vulnerable feelings of sadness, loneliness, and fear, a silent ache forms in the child's heart.

Processing emotions entails talking to an emotionally responsive adult about vulnerable feelings. Unable to process their vulnerable emotions, the child ultimately feels a bit less protected and a tad more troubled by the world.

The Big Three Vulnerable Emotions:
Sadness, Loneliness, Fear

Problems, real and significant, loom over families within the Yellow and Red Zones. The child knows they are loved, but does not feel it. Their capacity to endure frustration shrinks, and an ache for nurturing—a vague and nascent suffering—transmutes into diminished motivation and a compulsion to act out. Sibling cruelties, obnoxious behaviors, and back talk erupt more frequently, sadly eroding the joy once imagined of family life. Dramatic and frantic, the GOLDEN RETRIEVER parent is flummoxed about how to resolve unhappiness. There may be innumerable underlying reasons for a child's under-functioning or refusals.

It's important to understand a child wanders in a shadowland of invisible difficulties they can feel but often can't articulate.

> When a child plays the victim, projects blame, or continues to argue, it is an indication the child's capacity to face a situation is overwhelmed. The child needs more support and comfort to endure the challenge at hand.

Within this shadowland lies *situational* reasons for why a child may neglect responsibilities. Many reasons may not be apparent, such as needing additional time and emotional support to grieve the death of a pet, missing time with a parent who works late or who spends so much time with the new baby, or the echo of the word "divorce" overheard during his parents' heated argument the night before.

Equally important, there also may be personal reasons like ADHD, social anxiety, embarrassment over changing bodies, bullying, confusion about sexual or gender identity, and the list is infinite. (And no, dear Yellow Zone GOLDEN RETRIEVER parent, it's nothing you personally caused, but there is strategic parenting to make it better.)

Psychologically, a child with a heart wounded by sadness, loneliness, or fear has little recourse other than to resist the well-meaning expectations of others. To many caregivers, teachers, or coaches, however, the child may simply appear irresponsible, immature, or poorly behaved.

Within a distressed family, frustration and anger volley back and forth between parent and child; and within a turbulent home, pain gathers in the hearts of children. Young children form habits of intense and obnoxious behaviors in order to garner parental attention and connection; innately, understanding negative attention is better than no attention at all. Older children will do the same to avoid the burdens of responsibility. In both cases, insecurity bubbles in their guts, and children have no understanding of its origin.

To keep the emotional cauldron from boiling over in catastrophic intensity, distressed children develop very predictable reflexive defenses:

- Avoiding activities that normally would be enjoyable
- Blaming others for obvious self-failings
- Distracting themselves with media and devices to a harmful degree
- Fibbing in ways that seem senseless
- Instigating conflict with others to avoid feelings of failure

Though annoying, these defense mechanisms indicate the gripping pain that holds a child's tormented heart hostage.

PARTNERS OF THE STRESSED GOLDEN RETRIEVER PARENT

NURTURE

In co-parenting relationships, predictable patterns and problems emerge for each parenting style, especially under stress. Stress overwhelms parents, pushing them to the outer Yellow and Red Zones on the Map.

Remember, people typically choose partners opposite of themselves on the

Nurture Scale.[2] This means a GOLDEN RETRIEVER prefers to co-parent with Afghan Hounds or German Shepherds, both of whom tend to disengage from emotionally distressing situations over the long haul. Just when the GR feels neck-deep in the drama of family life, their mates often go AWOL, spiking feelings of resentment, rejection, or even abandonment.

Sadly and predictably, the GOLDEN RETRIEVER becomes preoccupied and overwhelmed under stress, while an Afghan Hound partner avoids and under-functions, and a German Shepherd partner becomes indignant and impatient.

In the Yellow and Red Zones, the GOLDEN RETRIEVER and the Afghan Hound pairing morph into the LOOSEY-GOOSEY parenting twosome. The GOLDEN RETRIEVER and German Shepherd become the COMMAND & RESCUE parenting duo.

Take a look at each parenting team under stress:

In the LOOSEY-GOOSEY parenting team, GOLDEN RETRIEVER and Afghan Hound, both caregivers are lax with family structure, and both tend to avoid conflict. A hallmark of this union is children who nip and bite the hand that feeds them by ignoring rules or overwhelming parental resolve with dramatic outbursts.

As far as family life goes, these partnerships become stressed and polarized. The Afghan Hound parent, once full of spontaneous optimism, now struggles to sustain resolve when it comes to rules and routines, while the GOLDEN RETRIEVER partner desperately strives to sustain structure with melodramatic flare-ups:

Here's an example of a LOOSEY-GOOSEY couple trying to plan the day:

AH: "There's only a half day of school today. Maddy says she's going to a matinee and wants some money but you won't give her any… you just yell at her."

GR: "I gave her money yesterday and now she wants more. I suppose she was crying and telling you how mean I am. I do everything around here and she never lifts a finger to help."

AH: "Well, what should I do? Should I tell her she can't go?"

GR: "What good will that do? She'll just find a way to do what she wants

---

[2] It is generally true opposites attract on the Nurture scale. The scope of this book on parenting does not intend to address the less frequent parenting patterns in which both partners fall on the same side of the Nurture Scale.

anyway. Why don't you just come home from work on time and cook dinner for once? It's not fair, I end up doing all the cooking. We both work full-time."

AH: "Okay, okay, okay. I'll take care of Maddy. You go ahead and go to work. I'll see you later tonight with your favorite Chinese takeout."

GR: "You don't get it. You just don't get it!!"

AH strides upstairs to scold Maddy…then gives her money for the show.

In this parenting team, flexing and bending can turn family structure into a three-ring circus of confusion.

Let's look at the COMMAND & RESCUE couple. In this pairing, the German Shepherd partner commands seemingly from on high, while the GOLDEN RETRIEVER parent rescues the children from their upset feelings. As the GR becomes emotionally preoccupied, the German Shepherd becomes emotionally distant or dismissive.

Each parent sees family problems differently. The GOLDEN RETRIEVER partner interprets behavioral problems as children needing more emotional warmth, and believes they are giving children more emotional support by being permissive with rules and expectations. The German Shepherd parent tends to see the problem in terms of children needing more discipline and consistency in the home, and becomes more commanding.

In the COMMAND & RESCUE partnership, each parent feels undermined and misunderstood, resulting in excruciating conversations that sound like this:

GR: "The kids sense we are not parenting as a team. They are always begging me to let them off some punishment you've given them."

GS: "If you would just enforce some of the rules around here, maybe the children would listen to you. Instead, you're always changing the rules. Kids need order and clear expectations."

GR: "Are you serious? The children basically hide from you because you are either yelling or lecturing them. For goodness sake, if you would just have some fun with them once in a while, maybe they wouldn't come running to me for everything."

GS: "Have *FUN* with the kids? They get anything and everything they want, because you give in to them. You're turning them into spoiled brats. They don't lift a finger to help out around here, and you think I should give them more FUN time?!"

And on it goes…good times, good times. This couple has quickly exited the Romeo and Juliet romantic stage of marriage and has belly-lopped into a *War of the Roses* melodrama.

HOPE FOR THE STRESSED GOLDEN RETRIEVER PARENT

Whether sad and overwhelmed or merely enduring chaotic family turmoil, there *is* hope for this compassionate parenting breed and the family. Their sense of empathy and kindness define all happy families, let alone caring communities.

The chapters ahead will help you and your family return to the Green Zone, where your children will happily reward your efforts with increased cooperation and you and your partner can gaze lovingly over a morning cup of coffee.

Quick Quiz

Golden Retriever Parents often suffer from:

a. Working too hard to make others happy

b. Resentments that grow due to too much self-sacrifice

c. Both the above

CHAPTER FOUR

The Border Collie Parenting Style

"Diligence is the mother of good luck."

BENJAMIN FRANKLIN

IF YOU HAVE TRACKED YOURSELF to the BORDER COLLIE quadrant of the Map, this chapter is for you. The BORDER COLLIE breed evolved and flourished along Scotland's stony highlands and grand glens. Here, sheepherders selectively bred this alert and energetic shepherding companion. How does your canine avatar translate to the furless family?

LETS TAKE A LOOK!

— — — — — — — — — — — — —

AT THEIR BEST, this parent attends to family life with vigilance and diligence and is unflagging while resolving problems.

AT THEIR WORST, this parent tends to micromanage and engage in power struggles and has fears of catastrophic outcomes.

DOMINANT BELIEF: if I don't do it … it won't get done.

LOVES to be involved and assist others when help is needed.

CO-PARENTING typically chooses a companion more relaxed about the daily details of family life: the AFGHAN HOUND or GERMAN SHEPHERD.

With perked ears, busily directing and herding children, this parenting style's dog tag reads:

PARENTING STRENGTHS IN ACTION

A round of applause and appreciative tip of the hat to the **BORDER COLLIE** parenting style. They embody the essence of active and engaged parenting. From chauffeuring teams of children in minivans to checking for incomplete homework assignments, these parents keep a tight flock. Few things please this parent more than watching over kids engaged in purposeful activities since they aver, "Idle hands are the devil's workshop."

This enthusiastic parent promotes worthwhile ventures, herds children away from hazards, and attends to sore hearts head-on when troubles sprout up. The **BORDER COLLIE** parenting style casts a wide net of care and course correction while guiding children through the rocky landscape of academic rigor, complicated friendships, and increasing responsibilities. Yup, this parenting style gets things done. Toss that pooch a treat!

At work, this attentive breed is often a top dog. In both corporate and entrepreneurial enterprises, the workplace environment hungers for this breed's conscientiousness.

LOCATION ON THE MAP

Let's take a moment to appreciate the highly responsive qualities of the **BORDER COLLIE** parenting style. The BC is found on the quadrant on the Map between COMFORT & FIRM.

Let's start with an in-depth look at the BORDER COLLIE on the Nurture Scale. Nurture Scale = How this parent responds to a child's feelings.

The **BORDER COLLIE** is most at home on the COMFORT end of the Nurture Scale.

BORDER COLLIES comfort by applying high sensitivity to distressed emotions in order to dissolve upset feelings and resolve the situation at hand. Ideally, parent and child feel and talk through the rough spots children come across nearly every day.

Toddler falls down, go boom? Best to guide him away from life's hard edges. Teen didn't make the varsity team? Better to talk through the disappointment and address the conditions that hobble success.

From classroom struggles to the loss of cherished friendships, children of the BC have access to the parent's bigger heart…and wisdom. Three cheers for this attentive breed!

> BORDER COLLIE and GOLDEN RETRIEVER parent styles both comfort. The GOLDEN RETRIEVER comforts with the purpose of healing the heart; the BORDER COLLIE with the purpose of fixing and moving on.

Let's look at the BORDER COLLIE parenting style on the Structure Scale. Structure Scale refers to the preferred manner of discipline \and teaching The 3Rs (Rules, Respect, and Responsibilities). The BORDER COLLIE is more comfortable on the FIRM end of the Structure Scale.

In the end, this fine breed uses consistent rules and routines to build structure in the home. Orderliness, believes the BC, fosters good habits, which leads to a solid character, and results in a successful life. In the mind of the BC, learning one's multiplication tables leads to… multiple job offers. Whereas, failure to master multiplication tables may lead to… repeating the fourth grade… or worse. Both the wish for achievement, as well as avoidance of catastrophic outcomes fuel the vim and vigor of this parenting style.

The BC's combined attributes of COMFORT & FIRM vigorously safeguard children who never feel neglected, though at times, may be annoyed by too much correction and advice.

Keep in mind that this FLEXIBLE & COMFORT tendency falls on a continuum. The BC parent can flex on household rules and will certainly encourage, but there will be a slight bias toward their natural style.

Let's take a quick look at a BC parent handling a child who is running late for school.

THE BORDER COLLIE, THE CHILD, AND THE SHOE

CHILD: "I can't find my other shoe! The bus is coming! Help me find my shoe!!"

BC: "Oh, no, again? Look on the doormat, and if it's not there, check your room."

CHILD: "Please, help me find it! The bus is coming! I don't want to be late again!"

BC: "I don't want you to be late either, honey. Here, wear these."

CHILD: "But, I hate those shoes!"

BC: "Tough luck kiddo, this is what we've got. Tonight, we'll find your shoes and put them where you'll find them in the morning."

What's going on in this example?

The child's upset feelings were touched on with sympathy, but were quickly nudged toward problem-solving. The BC parent believes dwelling on upset feelings simply bogs a person down from solving problems, and leaves one vulnerable.

ATTACHMENT THEORY AND THE BORDER COLLIE PARENT

Attachment Theory is the psychological school of thought that shows how children flourish and develop through attuned and connected attachment with their caregivers.

Children benefit from caregivers who:

1. *Encourage* them to explore

2. *Support* them while they persevere through roadblocks in their exploration, and

3. *Comfort* them in order they may recover from fatigue, upset feelings, and setbacks

> *Congrats, BORDER COLLIE! You SUPPORT children as they persevere in their efforts, and COMFORT them as they recover from fatigue and setbacks!*

As you might guess, the **BORDER COLLIE** parent is a natural when it comes to needed support and comfort (in the form of fixing). Aid, attention, and advice are deftly administered to keep children in line and on track, and, when needed, to calm upset feelings and fix problems.

BCs are less likely to permit risky adventures that lead to natural consequences and sharper lessons in life

Here's an example of a Border Collie parent in action:

Young Henry sits on the back steps, bored.

BC (supporting): "You okay, Henry? You're behind on your summer reading list. I'll get you a book."

HENRY: "Naw, I'm going to shoot some baskets. Some friends might come over to play."

Soon, a small group of kids are playing basketball in the driveway with sounds of laughter, squabbling about rules, and fairness, and whose foot did—or didn't—step out of bounds. Yelling and pushing breaks out between Henry and an older neighbor boy, and Henry begins to cry.

BC (comforting, in the form of fixing and managing): "Okay, that's enough. You can continue to play basketball, but first I'm gonna need you all to apologize and shake hands."

The BC parent unravels the knot of blame and excuses, eventually compelling the kids to comply.

BC: "I'll referee for a while, then you can get back to playing by yourselves."

Well done, **BORDER COLLIE** parent!

Henry was *supported* by the BC's attention to Henry's feelings of boredom. And later, the parent *comforts* by responding quickly and guiding children to manage disputes. As far as *encouraging*...well, this breed was thrown off the scent.

THE BORDER COLLIE'S PREFERRED METHOD OF GUIDING CHILDREN: COMPEL

Each of our four canine avatars has its own signature strategy of getting children to do what is expected of them. All parents use a variety of techniques to guide and motivate children, but each parent pooch has their own distinct method, especially when stressed. Here are the four primary strategies: the principled GERMAN SHEPHERD enforces, the compassionate GOLDEN RETRIEVER persuades, and the easygoing Afghan finesses. And, what about the attentive BORDER COLLIE? This parenting style's favored method is to compel.

> **com•pel** /kəm-'pel/ *verb*: the action to drive or to have an irresistible and powerful influence over another.

The three stages of *compel* are:

1. *Convince* with explanation and reminders

2. *Warn* about outcomes and consequences

3. *Coerce* by intensifying personal influence to ensure control and results

The BORDER COLLIE'S preferred method, compel, is similar to the GOLDEN RETRIEVER'S method, persuasion, but has more bite to it. Picture our diligent BORDER COLLIE on the Austrian hillside watching a flock of sheep. If a little lamb lags behind the flock…zoom, the passing blur of the BORDER COLLIE might convince him to get going and keep up. Yet, if our wee fella continues to wander in the wrong direction…*zing*: yapping and barking warns the woolgathering bundle of yarn to return to his baa-baa buddies. And if the mischievous mutton intentionally strays toward a yummy clover patch… *zowie:* a stinging nip on his tender flank, coerces our wayward lamb back to the fold.

From morning routines and getting to the bus on time to getting kids jammied, brushed, and ready for bed, the BORDER COLLIE caregiver is a vital and vibrant force: convincing the forgetful, warning the distracted, and coercing the stubborn.

We'll move now from the outback hillside of ravines and crispy clover to see how this parent breed might shepherd their little lamb in the family room:

BC (convince): "Jamar, it's time for piano practice. The recital is in a few weeks and your teacher wants you to show off your new skills. I know you don't want to sound bad in front of an audience."

JAMAR: "Later. I need a break from practice. I'm going to the park to hang with some friends."

BC (warn): "If you do poorly, nobody's going to be happy. Put some time in on the piano, then we can talk about you going to the park."

JAMAR: "Geez, it's my life. I can suck at the piano if I want to. I just want to see my friends for a while. Why are you so uptight all the time? My friend's parents are chill."

BC (coerce): "Practice for twenty minutes. You don't want to jeopardize your party plans this weekend, do you?"

JAMAR: "Are you seriously going to cancel the one fun thing I have to look forward to if I don't practice? Fine, I'll practice!"

In this scenario, the **BORDER COLLIE** parent is merely trying to prevent Jamar from wandering off, as little lambs are inclined to do. Too many things can go wrong in the BC's mind, things that could cause other problems to multiply. Problems such as a younger sibling refusing to do her lessons after seeing her older brother excused from his piano lesson; or Jamar refusing to attend the recital due to his failure to practice and fear of embarrassment.

The list of imagined calamities is often long. To prevent such unwelcome problems, the parent guides children with their compelling presence, keeping the family flock intact and away from a multitude of dangers unforeseen by others.

DIFFICULTIES FOR THE BORDER COLLIE PARENT

Being the attentive fixer in the company's IT department brings compliments and bonuses from bosses. But being an attentive fixer in the more murky, complex, and shifting world of family dynamics, well that's a special kind of difficulty. With an underlying fear of catastrophic outcomes, this parent may step too deep into problems, unintentionally treading on the child's feelings and inadvertently causing backlash.

In the above scenario, Jamar might transcend his upset feelings to find renewed dedication to piano practice. Let's hope so.

Or, Jamar might apathetically tinkle the ivories while brewing resentment toward this parent, which festers over time. A repeating cycle of parental frustration and child resistance is symptomatic of life in the troubled Yellow Zone, discussed ahead.

CO-PARENTING WITH A BORDER COLLIE PARENT

BORDER COLLIES tend to co-parent alongside people opposite their COMFORT orientation on the Nurture Scale. In other words, they typically pair up with a partner inclined to ENCOURAGE.

BCs are charmed by the cool, easygoing **AFGHAN HOUND** and envy their worry-free attitude. Or their heart races over the forthright and principled **GERMAN SHEPHERD** with admiration for their decisiveness and high standards.

The **BORDER COLLIE** parent typically becomes the alpha dog when it comes to managing family emotions with their committed and vigorous involvement in matters of both heart and home. Predictably, a common pattern emerges between co-parents. Over time, the BC assumes more and more of the childrearing responsibilities. And as long as the parenting team works toward fairness and balance, life bounces merrily along.

But as we all know, life presents us with an agility course of ups and downs, zigs and zags. Families endure accidents and illnesses. Adults care for aging parents while also raising children, juggling careers, and managing household budgets. New faces enter the scene when marriages dissolve.

These complications invite the **BORDER COLLIE** caregiver to take on more and more responsibilities. The tendency to over-function germinates a seed of discontent in the heart of this well-intentioned parent. Sit and stay for the upcoming segment on **BORDER COLLIES** in the cautionary Yellow and troubled Red Zones.

THE BORDER COLLIE PARENT IN THE TURBULENT YELLOW AND RED ZONES

Energetically guiding children toward success and feverishly herding them away from trouble…goodness, what could possibly go wrong for this parent? Well, a *lot* can go wrong, and with great intensity. Too much stress for too long morphs the BC's wonderfully attentive qualities into anxious circling, a tenacious presence, and overheated scrutiny of others.

In the Yellow Zone, the **BORDER COLLIE**'S cheerful, attentive nature distorts into preoccupation with managing others while neglecting their own vulnerable emotions. If left unchecked, the caregiver creeps into the realm of enmeshment, blurring interpersonal boundaries, and generating further conflict. Children react by under-functioning or pushing back.

In the Red Zone, the BC's controlling presence becomes pervasive. Chronic frustration overtakes the BC parent, building resistance in children. Eventually, a vicious cycle emerges as increasing opposition from the child unwittingly unleashes the BC's intense micromanager.

THE FRUSTRATION/RESISTANCE CYCLE

In a classic physics experiment, striking one tuning fork will cause a neighboring tuning fork to resonate at the same frequency. Frustration/ Resistance is the dynamic where a parent's visible frustration activates a child's resistance like two tuning forks resonating with each other. To understand its powerful influence over the emotions within the family, it deserves further exploration.

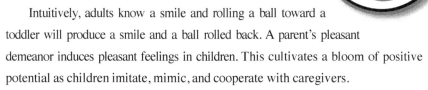

Intuitively, adults know a smile and rolling a ball toward a toddler will produce a smile and a ball rolled back. A parent's pleasant demeanor induces pleasant feelings in children. This cultivates a bloom of positive potential as children imitate, mimic, and cooperate with caregivers.

Less intuitive for caregivers is how an unpleasant parental interaction produces uncomfortable feelings in children. This spins a web of resistance toward their caregivers. When a parent uses an annoyed or irritable tone to send their child to bed, the child will undoubtedly whine and resist.

This hard-wired, psychosocial phenomenon exists within all social animals as they imitate, mimic, and attune to each other in a responsive, reflexive manner.

Frustration is the uncomfortable feeling that occurs when intentions are thwarted and expectations aren't met. Each day, parents have numerous intentions and expectations. They *intend* to go to work, make nutritional meals, and raise good children. And from dawn to dusk, they *expect* their kids to get up, get dressed, get out the door, do homework, and go to bed. When caregivers display frustration, the inevitable result is a child's resistance.

On a good day, a child may rise above their natural inclination to resist the demands of a frustrated adult and get ready before the bus comes. The parent may have banked enough goodwill to not trigger resistance, or, up to this point, the child has not had to endure multiple frustrations.

On a bad day, tolerance levels are depleted, and the child succumbs to the desire to resist— subconsciously landing a counter punch by stalling or arguing— and misses the bus.

In the Yellow and Red Zones, parental frustration and child resistance feed each other, spinning like a dog chasing its tail...and getting nowhere. This parent trap is called the Frustration/Resistance Cycle.

Spinning in a cycle of frustration and resistance more than occasionally throws families into the troubled Yellow and Red Zones, producing hungry hearts and hurt feelings. The ensuing flood of emotions swamps the BORDER COLLIE'S attentive capacity, leaving them frantically dog-paddling to control outcomes.

In the language of Attachment Theory, the BORDER COLLIE parent becomes preoccupied or enmeshed with others. In this state, the embattled BC begins to have difficulty emotionally separating from their children.

In addition to a deluge of emotions, the BORDER COLLIE'S tendency to think in terms of worst-case scenarios only fuels their tenacity. When a BC sees a child avoiding homework, it's not merely a poor grade to worry about. It's about the child failing school, and in just a few short years, living under a bridge eating beans out of a can. This may sound like an exaggeration, but for the BORDER

COLLIE'S reading this, most are wincing in self-recognition.

Here's an example of this force of nature in action:

STRESSED BC: "Remember, cello practice before going outside. Your teacher said, 'once a day, every day.' So get busy, Buster."

CHILD: "I practiced. You must have been outside or something."

STRESSED BC: "Nice try, but I know better. Your bow is right where you left it last night which, by the way, is not a safe place to put it."

CHILD: "Skipping one practice is not going to hurt. My teacher says I've got talent. Besides, it's my life. I wanna make my own decisions."

STRESSED BC: "I talked to your teacher yesterday, and she says your 'talent' is sneaking text messages to your friends during class. She also said you're falling behind. Jason's party is off limits until the practice gets done, and that means no video games either."

CHILD: "What?!! Why can't you just leave me alone and stop trying to control me? I can't have free time? I can't have friends? You call my teachers?! Why don't you get a life?! I'm not practicing, and I don't care about the stupid party!"

STRESSED BC: "Well, suit yourself. I'll call Jason's mom and tell her you won't be going to the party because you refuse to practice for a few minutes. Maybe if I ground you a couple days you'll get your priorities straight."

In the above example, this parent only wants what's best for the child. But the BORDER COLLIE'S tone and intensity alienate a child from a parent, leaving both with an anxious ache for each other. Both are stuck in a cycle of parental frustration and child resistance. Parent and child are like tuning forks resonating with each other, but attuned in emotional distress. When this happens, the child becomes less capable of facing the challenge of cello practice. Even if the BC wins the battle by compelling the child to practice, ultimately and sadly, the war is often lost. Resentment grows between parent and child, ensuring trouble in future encounters. In the Frustration/Resistance Cycle, the BC's wonderful attentiveness turns into anxious intrusiveness; driving others away.

As frustration and resistance continue between adults and children, it spreads and multiplies. Children realize their dramatic protests, relentless complaining, and persistent avoidance work, so they do more of it. Sooner or later, the child becomes intuitively aware of exactly what it will take for the parent to give in. Each mirrors the other in a twisting, downward spiral of irritated demands and angry protests known as the Frustration/ Resistance Cycle.

In the Green Zone, this type of interaction occurs only occasionally, in the Yellow Zone, regularly, and in the Red Zone, frequently. When this prickly pattern begins to grow, it's time to reach for help.

CHILDREN OF THE STRESSED BORDER COLLIE PARENT

When micromanaged by a stressed parent, children amp up resistance by ignoring or stalling, refusing requests, or nonstop arguing. By fifth grade, most children have discovered through trial and error, or intuition, which strategy works best and with which parent. This, by the way, is evidence of good emotional intelligence. The child has learned that evading or resisting the parent has a chance of derailing a BC. And at the very least—on a primal level—the child wishes to exact a cost to the parent for being unduly intrusive.

There are dark implications for children if families operate in the troubled Yellow and Red Zones for too long. Sure, children may avoid their responsibilities now and then. But in the long run, is this what they really need? Of course not. Parental disapproval and the child's failure to achieve The 3Rs (Rules, Respect, and Responsibilities) diminishes the child's self-esteem and capacity to handle the myriad tasks of childhood.

Of particular concern is the **BORDER COLLIE** parent becoming enmeshed, leading to children feeling crowded and micromanaged by the parent. Under this chaotic cloud, a child loses their connection to a calm and caring adult. The loss is twofold. First, there is a generalized disruption of emotional stability. Second, the child loses the ability to process emotions. When children are unable to fully share their intense feelings of frustration and anger, or their vulnerable feelings of sadness, loneliness, and fear, a silent ache forms in the child's heart.

The Big Three Vulnerable Emotions: **Sadness, Loneliness, Fear**

Processing emotions entails talking to an emotionally receptive adult about vulnerable feelings. Unable to process their vulnerable emotions, the child ultimately feels a bit less protected and a tad more troubled by the world.

Problems real and significant loom over families within the Yellow and Red zones. The child knows they are loved, but does not feel it. Their capacity to endure frustration shrinks. An ache for nurturing—a vague and nascent suffering—transmutes into diminished motivation and a compulsion to act out. Sibling cruelties, obnoxious behaviors, and back talk erupt more frequently, sadly eroding the love once imagined of family life. Doggedly engaged but fatigued, the BORDER COLLIE parent is flummoxed about how to resolve unhappiness.

There may be innumerable underlying reasons for a child's under-functioning or refusals. It's important to understand a child swims in a shadowland of invisible difficulties they can feel but often can't articulate.

Within this shadowland lies *situational* reasons for why a child may neglect responsibilities. Many reasons may not be apparent, such as needing additional time and emotional support to grieve the death of a pet, missing time with a parent who works late or who spends so much time with the new baby, or the echo of the word "divorce" overheard during his parents' heated argument the night before.

Equally important, there may also be personal reasons like ADHD, social anxiety, embarrassment over changing bodies, bullying, confusion about sex and gender identity, and the list is infinite. (And no, dear Yellow Zone BORDER COLLIE parent, this is not just dwelling on sadness.)

Psychologically, a child with a heart burdened by sadness, loneliness, or fear has little recourse other than to resist the well-meaning expectations of others. To many caregivers, coaches, or teachers however, the child may simply appear irresponsible, immature, or poorly behaved.

Within a distressed family, frustration and anger volley back and forth between parent and child; and within a turbulent home, pain gathers in the hearts of children. Young children form habits of intense and obnoxious behaviors in order to garner parental attention and connection; innately, understanding negative attention is better than no attention at all. Older children will do the same to avoid the burdens of responsibility. In either case, insecurity bubbles in their guts, and children have no understanding of its origin.

To keep the emotional cauldron from boiling over in catastrophic intensity, distressed children develop very predictable strategies of resistance:

- Avoiding activities that normally would be enjoyable
- Blaming others for obvious self-failings
- Distracting themselves with media and devices to a harmful degree
- Fibbing in ways that seem senseless
- Instigating conflict with others to avoid feelings of failure

These strategies, though worrisome and maddening to a parent, often reveal a reign of heartache that holds captive the child's beleaguered heart.

PARTNERS OF THE STRESSED BORDER COLLIE PARENT

Opposites Attract Along the Nurture Scale

In co-parenting relationships, predictable patterns and problems emerge for each parenting style, especially under stress. Stress overwhelms parents, pushing them to the outer Yellow and Red Zones on the Map. Remember, people choose partners opposite of themselves on the Nurture Scale. This means a BORDER COLLIE tends to co-parent with German Shepherds and Afghan Hounds.

Sadly and predictably, the frantic BORDER COLLIE becomes preoccupied and controlling under stress, while a German Shepherd partner becomes impatient and indignant, and an Afghan Hound partner becomes under-functioning and avoidant.

In the Yellow and Red Zones, the BORDER COLLIE and the Afghan Hound become the GOOD COP/BAD COP parenting team. The BORDER COLLIE and German Shepherd couple become the RIGHT & TIGHT parenting duo. Let's take a look at each parenting team under stress.

In a GOOD COP/BAD COP pairing, the conflict-averse Good Cop Afghan Hound and the enforcer Bad Cop BORDER COLLIE square off. Power struggles between the BORDER COLLIE parent and children generate emotional heat and turmoil. The Afghan Hound—inclined to engage with sunny emotions and steer clear of stormy ones—retreats into their own world. Whether it's work, hobbies, or something else, the AH seeks a modicum of positive engagement outside of the family. The predictable marital result? The BC fumes about feeling abandoned. The AH retreats further. The BC amps up, and the AH retreats further still. Stress and anxiety have everybody reeling.

The stressed GOOD COP/BAD COP relationship ends up sounding something like this:

AH: "I gave Maya permission to go to the skating party tonight."

BC: "What?! She's behind on homework. Yesterday she told me to shut up and I grounded her for it. You have to check with me about these things."

AH: "Hey, all she wants to do is get out of the house and have fun like a normal kid. It's not like she's failing fourth grade, you know. She wanted to tell you, but she was afraid you'd throw a fit."

BC: "Seriously? Why do I always have to be the bad guy while you do as you damn well please, undermining me... going behind my back? You let her have her way so she'll like you. Well, that's being her friend, not her parent!"

AH: "Wow, no wonder Maya wants to get away from you. You're so damned controlling, nobody can stand being around you. You and Maya go ahead and keep yelling at each other. I'm going to clean the gutters!"

This kind of marital stress may seem innocuous, like a tempest in a teacup. But the subtle hostility of family life puts a spear point to every quarrel and a burr to every word.

The RIGHT & TIGHT couple is made up of a stressed BORDER COLLIE with another FIRM parenting style, a stressed German Shepherd. This household operates on the right principles and tight management. Both the BORDER COLLIE and German Shepherd parenting styles prefer FIRM structure, and each willingly to tug the leash when rearing children.

The BC delivers discipline in a flurry of attentiveness, advice, and reminders, while the GS episodically steps in to redirect, scold, lecture, or impose punishment; often with impatience and anger. Coming from both parents, a tyranny of guidance causes kids to feel collared, critiqued, and curtailed; and ultimately less functional. Under these circumstances, it is easy for parents to lose track of a child's heart.

Exchanges between the RIGHT & TIGHT parents sound something like this:

GS: "Maya asked about going to the mall Friday night. I said no, she had homework to do. She started whining, so I grounded her for the weekend."

BC: "You grounded her for whining?"

GS: "I grounded her for using high drama in order to dodge her homework again. I want her to learn there are consequences for that kind of behavior."

BC: "Well, she's struggling with science. I'll turn off the WiFi and make sure she reads her textbook. Please, don't raise your voice at her anymore tonight. I'll make sure things get done."

In the scenario above, neither the BORDER COLLIE nor the German Shepherd will allow Maya to go to the mall. The German Shepherd will be the first to implement the restriction, and the BORDER COLLIE will take over the management of the rule, essentially to protect the child from the German Shepherd parent's drill sergeant-like manner.

THE HOSTILE DEPENDENT RELATIONSHIP

Naturally dependent on caregivers, children resonate with expressions of appreciation and compassion. Conversely, a child who has accumulated a heart filled with hurt will reflexively express hostility or resentment toward the caregiver. This anger triggers frustration in a controlling parent, setting the Frustration/ Resistance Cycle in motion. The child forms a relationship with the parent that is both hostile and dependent.

Another scenario with this parenting team is while parental expectations drive children to strive, the steep gradient of constantly succeeding fatigues them. When children begin to falter due to the mounting pressure of both social functioning and performance expectations, it's time to seek help.

HOPE FOR THE STRESSED BORDER COLLIE PARENT

Whether frantic and frustrated, anxious and critical, or merely fatigued by family failures, there is hope for this alert and eager parenting breed…and the family. For it must be noted that the family needs them. Their sense of vigilance and protection, their respect for responsibility, and cooperation are critical attributes of happy families. But how to get back to the Green Zone so these wonderful attributes can flourish?

If you are co-parenting, read the section describing your partner's parenting style. After that, skip ahead to Section III: The Three Stage Path to Harmony with steps on healing your family.

Quick Quiz

A typical personal growth area for the BC Style is:

a. Securing a refillable muscle relaxant medication

b. Mindfulness and Yoga training to settle stress and catastrophic ideas

c. Continue to control all things all the time until people with white coats arrive

CHAPTER FIVE

The German Shepherd Parenting Style

"The first rule in this house is discipline."

CAPTAIN VON TRAPP

IF YOU TRACKED your parenting style to the GERMAN SHEPHERD, this chapter is for you! Assisting generations of sheep herders throughout the European continent, the GERMAN SHEPHERD evolved as a preferred companion. Smart and hardworking, protective and courageous, this dutiful breed and parenting style preserves order and defends boundaries. How does your canine avatar translate to the two-legged parenting world?

LET'S TAKE A LOOK!

— — — — — — — — — — — — — —

AT THEIR BEST, this parent is principled and loyal to ideas and causes, rules and responsible behavior. They exude calm and stability to family life.

AT THEIR WORST, this parent becomes commanding, impatient, or angry; isolates from others with a self-righteous attitude which can appear dismissive to others; and is prone to feeling lonely.

DOMINANT BELIEFS: there are consequences, both positive and negative, to behavior, and children must learn from those consequences. Work comes before play.

LOVES to live by and instill values and virtues that promote responsibility and achievement.

CO-PARTNERING: chooses partners more emotionally attentive than themselves: GOLDEN RETRIEVERS and BORDER COLLIES.

The GERMAN SHEPHERD parent instills virtues and good character in children. For these reasons, this breed's dog tag reads :

PARENTING STRENGTHS IN ACTION

A crisp salute to the **GERMAN SHEPHERD** parent. As the coaches and den leaders of the community, they serve similar roles in the family. Teaching morality lessons, the discipline of honing skills, and the preparedness expounded in scouting, all appeal to this parent.

GS caregivers desire to impart important life lessons to children, leading them on a path to success in the classroom, ballfields, and beyond. Sure, a whimsical bedtime story is well and good, but a How-To book is more useful. And while a game of UNO is exciting, a strategic game of chess or physical sport is even better. These parents engage children in fun activities, like all parents do, but usually with an underlying instructive purpose. There are lessons to learn, rules to follow, and clear expectations to meet while growing into well-adjusted children. A pat on the head for this noble breed!

These attributes, full of boundaries and self-discipline, serve the business world well. Not surprisingly, most airline pilots and surgeons who walk through my office door identify as **GERMAN SHEPHERD** parents.

LOCATION ON THE MAP

Let's pause to ponder the sturdy psyche of the **GERMAN SHEPHERD** parenting style. The GS is found on the quadrant on the Map between ENCOURAGE & FIRM.

The GERMAN SHEPHERD'S strength on the Nurture Scale is encouragement.

This caregiver employs attributes of leadership discipline. The GS's confident emotional demeanor draws children toward fuller participation in life. From a child's first steps and first words, to sports and clarinet practice, all are driven by the spark of encouragement. Encouragement electrifies interest, amps up motivation, and switches on focus. As a result, children transcend setbacks that threaten achievement.

Toddler falls down, go boom? Best to set him on his feet to try again. Teen didn't make the varsity team? Better schedule more practice time, "You can do anything you want, kiddo; it just takes time, practice, and hard work!" Three cheers for encouragement in action!

GERMAN SHEPHERD and AFGHAN HOUND parent types both sit on the encourage side of the scale. The GERMAN SHEPHERD encourages with conventional wisdom and leadership while the AFGHAN HOUND encourages with spontaneity and relaxed engagement.

Let's look at our pack leader parent on the Structure Scale, where discipline and the The 3Rs (Rules, Respect, and Responsibility) are taken seriously. In short, the GS takes structure seriously. Instilling good habits and skills gives children a leg up in a demanding and competitive world, so it's worth a dustup now and then for the GS to enforce the rules. You'll likely hear this caregiver use adages such as "Work before play," "Your word is your honor," and "Practice makes perfect."

The 3Rs

Rules
Respect
Responsibility

These phrases reinforce consistent boundaries that prevent children from straying too far. And if they do wander off? Well, consequences and further expectations will guide them back into line.

*The GS's combined attributes of
ENCOURAGE & FIRM confidently
shepherd children toward success…
whether children are fully willing or not.*

Keep in mind this ENCOURAGE & FIRM parenting tendency falls on a continuum. The GS parent can flex on household rules, and certainly will comfort, but there will be a slight bias toward their natural style.

Let's take a quick look at a GS parent handling a child who is running late for school:

THE GERMAN SHEPHERD, THE CHILD, AND THE SHOE

CHILD: "I can't find my shoes! The bus is coming! Help!!"

GS: "Sorry, Hon. Better hurry up and find them. The bus isn't going to wait for you. Try to remember where you put them."

CHILD: "Somebody moved them! It's not my fault!"

GS: "No one else wears your shoes. Think where you were when you took them off last."

CHILD (quietly tears up): "Never mind. I'll find them myself."

What's going on in this example? In this account, the GS's attention focuses on responsibility and allows the child to face natural consequences, such as possibly missing the bus. This parent barely touches on the child's feelings and moves toward what seems to them to be the core issues: acting responsibly and problem-solving. Notably missing are the warmer tones of sympathy, indicative of a comforting parent style, who typically responds first with sympathy and offers of help.

ATTACHMENT THEORY AND THE GERMAN SHEPHERD PARENT

Attachment Theory is the psychological school of thought that shows how children flourish and develop through attuned and connected attachment with their caregivers.

Children benefit from caregivers who:

1. *Encourage* them to explore,

2. *Support* them while they persevere through roadblocks in their exploration, and

3. *Comfort* them so they recover from fatigue, upset feelings, and setbacks.

Congrats, GERMAN SHEPHERD! You ENCOURAGE children to explore and SUPPORT them as they persevere in their efforts!

As you might guess, the **GERMAN SHEPHERD** parents may be a bit awkward or disinclined toward comforting, but they are great at getting children out and involved in healthy and worthwhile endeavors.

Here's an example of a **GERMAN SHEPHERD** parent in action:

Young Henry sits on the back steps, kinda bored.

GS: "Hey Henry, let's shoot some hoops…work on your jump shots and free throws."

HENRY: "Aw, I don't know…"

GS (encourage): "Come on, let's polish up our skills a bit. Maybe some other kids will join us!"

The two of them go to the driveway to dribble and shoot. Pretty soon, as the parent predicted, neighborhood kids join in. Our GS coaxes and coaches the game, guiding them toward good sportsmanship and proper technique. The kids learn more about the game. Then, there's some pushing and shoving, and Henry hurts his ankle.

HENRY: "Max won't play fair. I don't want to play anymore!"

GS: "It looked like an accident to me."

HENRY: "It wasn't an accident! He fouled me. He's always shoving and pushing, and you never call foul!"

GS: "You gotta learn to play against all sorts of players, Buddy. Quitting isn't the answer. How about you focus on your own game."

Henry stomps off in frustration while our GS parent waits holding the ball. After a few minutes, Henry agrees to rejoin the game.

Well done, **GERMAN SHEPHERD** parent! Henry got outside, the game got going, and in this scenario, Henry endured through his pain and frustration in order to persevere. In terms of wanting someone to attend to his upset feelings…well, Henry is barking up the wrong tree.

THE GERMAN SHEPHERD'S PREFERRED METHOD OF GUIDING CHILDREN: ENFORCE

Each of our four canine avatars has their own signature strategy of getting children to do what is expected of them. All parents use a variety of methods to guide and motivate children, but each parent pooch has their own distinct method, especially when stressed. Here are the four primary strategies: the compassionate GOLDEN RETRIEVER persuades, the attentive BORDER COLLIE compels, and the easygoing Afghan finesses. And what of the GERMAN SHEPHERD parent? This parenting style's favored method is to enforce.

> **en•force** /in'fôrs,en'fôrs/ *verb*: compel observance of or compliance with a law, rule, or obligation.

The three stages of *enforce* are:

    1. Set expectations

    2. *Explain* (aka "The Lecture")

    3. Apply or allow *consequences*

Setting expectations appeals to a child's sense of responsibility while also implying a sense of authority by the parent. It can be seen as a form of leadership.

When the GS *explains,* it's expressing their resolve, providing reasoning and implications about the child's behavior. In a sense, it's an appeal to the child's higher mind.

The GERMAN SHEPHERD's willingness to apply consequences is a form of respect for the child, knowing the child's decisions are allowed as long as the child knows what the consequences might be. The GS finds gratification in the child learning from consequences. In the mind of the GS, it's the way the world, and the best learning, works.

Here's an example of the GS's ENFORCE method in play:

A GERMAN SHEPHERD parent unleashes his thirteen-year-old daughter and two of her friends at FunLand Amusement Park while he gets some work done at a coffee shop.

GS (sets expectations): "Okay, Jocelyn, I'll see you right here in exactly two hours. Here's thirty dollars. That's all you get. Spend it wisely."

Forty minutes later, Jocelyn returns with a poster sticking out of her backpack, a plush toy clipped to her belt loop, and sipping a chocolate milkshake.

JOCELYN: "Wow, Dad, everything is so expensive here! Can I have a little more money? You can take it out of my next allowance."

GS (explaining): "Remember when we arrived, Jocelyn? I warned you that thirty dollars was all you'd get. This has happened before, and I know your mom helps you out. But we are done with that now. It's time you learn money doesn't grow on trees. You need to realize how much things cost and plan ahead.

JOCELYN: "I don't even know what you're talking about! I just want to have fun today! Daddy, please, my friends are waiting!!"

GS (applying consequences): "I'm sorry, Jocelyn. I told you you'd only get thirty dollars. End of discussion."

JOCELYN: "But I won't be able to go on any of the rides with my friends! I'll pay you back!!"

GS: (allowing consequences with a little more lecture): "I know you're angry, honey, but one day, you'll thank me for teaching you to be responsible. FunLand will still be here when you get your next allowance. You're lucky you have a dad that loves you too much to spoil you."

JOCELYN: "WhatEVERRR!!!"

In our example, Jocelyn's pleas and protests bounce right off the GS's principled heart. Jocelyn is forced to learn from the consequences of her decisions. Mission accomplished. Children prosper under established boundaries and The 3Rs (Rules, Respect, and Responsibilities). Discipline creates habits that form good character. And that's what the GERMAN SHEPHERD parent is all about.

DIFFICULTIES FOR THE GERMAN SHEPHERD PARENT

For encouraging to be effective, a child must be in a certain state of mind. They must be ready and willing—or at least neutral about—the parent *and* the situation at hand. For example, a rosy-cheeked, well-rested, and cheerful kid needs little encouragement from a parent to help with some house or yard work.

On the other hand, a bleary-eyed, fatigued, and sullen child is impervious to encouragement—and will resist unless and until the child's problems of the heart are settled first. If these problems are fairly typical and obvious, as in the Green Zone, the GS will most likely sort it out using their secondary strengths of being *flexible* and *empathetic* to the child's distress. If the GS persists with attempts to encourage a resistant child by ramping up the firmness, the distressed child will resist or refuse in one form or another.

In the example of Jocelyn at the amusement park, children will learn from consequences *as long as* there is enough overall emotional support for children to endure upset feelings of sadness and frustration. In other words, young Jocelyn will accept and learn from her embarrassing shortage of money if, in the long run, she feels emotionally supported by her GS father. Emotional support sounds something like this, "I'm sorry you ran out of money, honey. I know it's frustrating. But I love you too much to not help you learn money management."

Without a positive balance in the emotional support account, Jocelyn will simply blame him for being stupid, mean, or cheap.

Within the expanse of a parent's loving presence, a child is able to endure the vexation of learning important life lessons.

But what happens for the GS when this balance is out of whack when enforcement strategies and impatience outweigh empathetic support? Well, that's a GS in the Yellow or Red Zone, something we'll talk about after a quick note on co-parenting.

CO-PARENTING WITH A GERMAN SHEPHERD PARENT

As a partner, the GS has incontestable appeal: stalwart, reliable, goal-oriented, and loyal. More reasoned than emotional, they tend to attract, and be attracted to, more emotionally expressive partners; their opposites on the Nurture Scale. In other words, GERMAN SHEPHERD parent types pant over GOLDEN RETRIEVERS or BORDER COLLIES. So yes, opposites on the Nurture Scale absolutely attract!

Often faltering in the language of love themselves, the regimented GS seeks and enjoys the emotional availability of their spouses. From Maria and Georg Von Trapp in the classic *The Sound of Music* to the self-help exploration of love by John Grey's *Men Are From Mars, Women Are From Venus,* this formula of attraction is reflected throughout our culture.

We will peek at some cringe-worthy misunderstandings that spin off from this intense coupling, as we look at the GS in... *da da da dum:* the troubled Yellow and Red Zones.

THE GERMAN SHEPHERD PARENTS IN THE TURBULENT YELLOW AND RED ZONES

A principled parent who assertively enforces rules and expectations... goodness, what could go wrong? Well, quite a bit can go wrong; and, often, with irksome glares and strident voices.

In the Yellow Zone, the GS's encouragement falters with stressed children. The parent's fortitude shifts to impatience. If left unchecked, the caregiver creeps further toward irritability and self-righteousness, marching directly toward the Red Zone.

In the Red Zone, the GS's commanding presence generates fear and mounting resentment in children. A mental state of dismissiveness toward the feelings of others and disengagement from mutual understanding leaves this well-intentioned parent barking out orders or retreating to the doghouse when sensing something is wrong.

THE FRUSTRATION/RESISTANCE CYCLE

In a classic physics experiment, striking one tuning fork will cause a neighboring tuning fork to resonate at the same frequency. Frustration/ Resistance Cycle is the dynamic where a parent's visible frustration activates a child's resistance like two tuning forks resonating with each other. To understand its powerful influence over the emotions within the family, it deserves further exploration.

Intuitively, adults know a smile and rolling a ball toward a toddler will produce a smile and a ball rolled back. A parent's pleasant demeanor induces pleasant feelings in children. This cultivates a bloom of positive potential as children imitate, mimic, and cooperate with caregivers.

Less intuitive for caregivers is how an unpleasant parental interaction produces uncomfortable feelings in children. This spins a web of resistance toward their caregivers. When a parent uses an annoyed or irritable tone to send their child to bed, the child will undoubtedly whine and resist.

*A hard-wired, psychosocial phenomenon
exists within all social animals as they
imitate, mimic, and attune to each other in
a responsive, reflexive manner.*

Frustration is the uncomfortable feeling that occurs when intentions are thwarted, and expectations aren't met. Each day, parents have numerous intentions and expectations. They *intend* to go to work, make nutritional meals, and raise good children. And from dawn to dusk, they *expect* their kids to get up, get dressed, get out the door, do homework, and go to bed. When caregivers display frustration, the inevitable result is a child's resistance.

On a good day, a child may rise above their natural inclination to resist the demands of a frustrated adult and get ready before the bus comes. The parent may have banked enough goodwill to not trigger resistance or, up to this point, the child has not had to endure multiple frustrations.

On a bad day, tolerance levels are depleted, and the child succumbs to the desire to resist— subconsciously landing a counterpunch by stalling or arguing— and misses the bus.

In the Yellow and Red Zones, parental frustration and child resistance feed each other; spinning like a dog chasing its tail…and getting nowhere. This parent trap is called the Frustration/Resistance Cycle.

The troubled Yellow and Red Zones generate hungry hearts and hurt feelings. When resistance grows in the heart of a child, the **GERMAN SHEPHERD'S** strong-suit of encouragement becomes less and less effective, and even counterproductive.

Encouraging a reluctant or resistant child generates resentment and anger. Eventually, and unfortunately, stress amplifies the GS's authoritarian tendencies and the Frustration/ Resistance Cycle spins into high gear. *Woof!*

In the language of Attachment Theory, this parent type becomes dismissive of the upset feelings of those around them.

Children respond in kind. They dodge family engagement. They avoid, blame, and ignore the parent. Of course, this is not a formula for peaceful cooperation with children.

A frustrated GS parent engaging with a resistant child sounds something like this:

GS: "Shut off the computer and grab your gear, it's time for hockey practice."

FRANNIE: " I don't want to go. I'm tired.

GS: "That doesn't matter. You signed up to play hockey; you practice. It's not about you. It's about the team. Now go get your equipment."

FRANNIE: "I hate hockey! The coach never puts me in the game, anyway. I'm not going. I'm quitting!"

GS: "The heck you are! It's doesn't matter if you like it. You made a commitment and I paid good money for all this. I'm serious, stop being lazy and GET YOUR BAG!"

FRANNIE: "Mom, Dad's yelling at me!"

In the above example, the child doesn't *intend* to be bratty, nor does the parent *intend* to nag. Both are stuck in the spin cycle of parental frustration and child resistance. Parent and child are like tuning forks resonating with each other, but attuned in emotional distress.

When this happens, the child is less likely to be able to face the challenge of practice. In order to change the situation, the parent must lead so the child will follow.

The GS is simply trying to be a good parent but with disappointing results. The GS encourages Frannie to do the right thing. But he delivers the message on the values of participation and following through on commitments in the form of scolding and lecturing: classic Yellow Zone stuff for the GS. For whatever reason, the child is not ready and willing to go to practice.

In the scenario above, even if the GS wins the battle by coercing the child into going to hockey practice, ultimately and sadly, the war is often lost. Children learn to avoid the stressed GS parent, who frequently becomes the loneliest of all four of our parenting styles.

In the Frustration/Resistance Cycle, children refuse—or sabotage the activity —to steer clear of the episodically angry GS parent. Even fun activities are avoided or simply fall apart. The GS's wonderful gifts of principled living and adventurous learning are rejected, as their authoritarian manner drives others away.

As frustration and resistance continue between adults and children, it spreads and multiplies. Children begin to realize their dramatic protests, relentless complaining, and persistent avoidance work, so they do more of it. Sooner or later, the child becomes intuitively aware of exactly what it will take for the parent to give in. Each mirrors the other in a twisting, downward spiral of demands and angry protests known as the Frustration/Resistance Cycle.

In the Green Zone, this type of interaction occurs occasionally, in the Yellow Zone, regularly, and in the Red Zone, frequently. When this prickly pattern grows, it's time to reach for help.

CHILDREN OF THE STRESSED GERMAN SHEPHERD PARENT

A stressed GS barks out orders in a harsh tone of voice that the child interprets as disdain. Feeling disliked or unloved, the parent's frustration ignites resistance, and the child reflexively resolves to do anything other than cooperate with someone who holds no affection for them. As a result, the child of a stressed **GERMAN SHEPHERD** may agree to do the assigned task but is likely to ignore the request or leave the job half-finished.

Alternatively, the child might go to the other parent and whine, beg, or cry to get out of complying. By fifth grade, most children—through trial and error, or intuition, have discovered which strategy works best and with which parent. This, by the way, is evidence of emotional intelligence.

Dark implications arise for children if families operate in the troubled Yellow and Red Zones for too long. Sure, children may avoid their responsibilities now and then. But in the long run, is this what they really need? Of course not. Parental disapproval and the child's failure to achieve The 3Rs (Rules, Respect, and Responsibilities) diminishes the child's self-esteem and capacity to handle the myriad of tasks in childhood.

Of particular concern is the **GERMAN SHEPHERD** parent becoming forcefully authoritarian. Instead of protecting and shielding the hearts of their children, the stressed GS may default to wielding intimidation and eliciting fear.

There is a deeper problem for children of the stressed GS parent. Once the cycle of command and control meets a child's unhappiness and resistance, there is no place to go other than conflict. Feeling unloved and unworthy the child will avoid or defy this parent while at the same time strongly ache for their approval.

Under this chaotic cloud children feel alienated from their parent's love and acceptance, losing their connection to a calm and caring adult. The dilemma is twofold. First, there is a generalized disruption of emotional stability and, secondly, a diminishment in the ability to process emotions. When children are unable to fully share their intense feelings of frustration and anger, or their vulnerable feelings of sadness, loneliness and fear, a silent ache forms in the child's heart.

The Big Three Vulnerable Emotions: **Sadness, Loneliness, Fear**

Processing emotions entails talking to an emotionally receptive adult about vulnerable feelings. Unable to process their vulnerable emotions, the child ultimately feels a bit less protected and a tad more troubled by the world.

Problems real and significant loom over families within the Yellow and Red Zones. The child knows they are loved but does not feel it. Their capacity to endure frustration shrinks, and an ache for nurturing—a vague and nascent suffering—transmutes into diminished motivation and a compulsion to act out. Sibling cruelties, obnoxious behaviors, and back talk erupt more frequently, sadly eroding the love once imagined of family life. Estranged and embittered, the GERMAN SHEPHERD parent is flummoxed about how to resolve conflict and unhappiness.

There may be innumerable underlying reasons for a child's under-functioning or refusals. It's important to understand a child swims in a shadowland of invisible difficulties they can feel but often can't articulate.

Within this shadowland lies situational reasons for why a child may neglect responsibilities. Many reasons may not be apparent, such as needing additional time and emotional support to grieve the death of a pet, missing time with a parent who works late or who spends so much time with the new baby, or the echo of the word "divorce" overheard during his parent's heated argument the night before.

Equally important, there may also be personal reasons like ADHD, social anxiety, embarrassment over changing bodies, bullying, confusion about sex and gender identity, and the list is infinite. (And no, dear GERMAN SHEPHERD parent, more tough-love will not solve these issues.)

Psychologically, a child with a heart wounded by sadness, loneliness, or fear has little recourse other than to resist the well-meaning expectations of others. To many caregivers, coaches, or teachers, however, the child may simply appear irresponsible, immature, or poorly behaved.

Within a distressed family, frustration and anger echo back and forth between parent and child, and within a turbulent home, pain gathers in the hearts of children. Young children form habits of intense and obnoxious behaviors in order to establish a parental connection, innately understanding negative attention is better than no attention at all. Older children will do the same to avoid the burdens of responsibility. In both cases, insecurity bubbles in their guts, and children have no understanding of its origin.

To keep the emotional cauldron from boiling over in catastrophic intensity, distressed children develop very predictable strategies of resistance:

- Avoiding activities that normally would be enjoyable
- Blaming others for obvious self-failings
- Distracting themselves with media and devices to a harmful degree
- Fibbing in ways that seem senseless
- Instigating conflict with others to avoid feelings of failure

Though annoying for caregivers, these defense mechanisms indicate the gripping pain that holds a child's tormented heart hostage.

When a child plays the victim, projects blame, or continues to argue, it is an indication the child's capacity to face a situation is overwhelmed. The child needs more support and comfort to endure the challenge at hand.

PARTNERS OF THE STRESSED GERMAN SHEPHERD PARENT

Regarding co-parenting relationships, predictable patterns and problems emerge for each parent type, especially under stress. Stress overwhelms parents, pushing them to the outer Yellow and Red Zones on the Map.

Remember, people choose partners opposite of themselves on the Nurture Scale. This means **GERMAN SHEPHERDS** tend to co-parent with **Border Collies** and **Golden Retrievers**.

Sadly and predictably, the **GERMAN SHEPHERD** becomes impatient and indignant under stress, while the **Border Collie** partner becomes controlling, and the **Golden Retriever** partner becomes overwhelmed.

In the Yellow and Red Zones, the **GERMAN SHEPHERD** and the **Golden Retriever** pairing becomes the COMMAND & RESCUE couple. The **GERMAN SHEPHERD** and **Border Collie** become the RIGHT & TIGHT couple. Let's take a look at each parenting team under stress.

In the COMMAND & RESCUE situation, the **GERMAN SHEPHERD** parent commands seemingly from on high, while the **Golden Retriever** parent rescues children from their upset feelings. As the **GERMAN SHEPHERD** becomes emotionally distant or dismissive, the **Golden Retriever** becomes emotionally preoccupied.

Each parent sees family problems differently. A **GERMAN SHEPHERD** parent interprets family problems as children needing more consistency and discipline and, therefore, becomes more commanding. In response, the **Golden Retriever** partner interprets problems as children needing more emotional warmth and rescues them by being permissive to rules and expectations.

In the COMMAND & RESCUE partnership, each parent feels undermined and misunderstood, resulting in excruciating conversations like this:

GS PARENT: "Listen, we need some consistency around here. Bedtime is 9:00 p.m., and whenever I try to enforce it, you let the kids have more time. It makes me the bad guy."

GR PARENT: "They just want to spend some quality time with us. Everyone is so busy all day. It's our only time together. Besides, it's the only time you're not barking at them to do something."

GS PARENT: "Are you serious? The only reason I yell at them is because you keep letting them get away with things. There's no routine; no consistency. Why do you make excuses for them? They're getting lazy."

GR PARENT: "Wow, the way you talk about your own children! No wonder they vanish whenever you're around. They feel like you don't even like them!"

GS PARENT: "Forget it. Do what you want. Let them stay up until midnight. Hell, let them stay home from school and bake cookies all day! I'm going to bed. I have work in the morning."

Cupid's arrows are flying awry for this couple, poking each other in the eye rather than stirring the heart. Sadly, this kind of conversation frequently erupts for **GERMAN SHEPHERD** and **Golden Retriever** couples in the Yellow and Red Zones. Children suffer uniquely as they juggle mixed messages, flared tempers, as well as insecurity about whether the family will simply survive.

The RIGHT & TIGHT scenario is comprised of a stressed **GERMAN SHEPHERD** with another FIRM parenting style, a stressed **Border Collie**. This household is run by the right principles and tight management. This powerful partnering is defined by order, rules, and expectations. With nurturing sprinkled sparingly along the outer edges, this couple in the Yellow Zone or Red Zone starves a child's heart. During times of family difficulties, an indignant GS cracks the whip for rule and order while at the same time defaulting on expressions of care and comfort.

Meanwhile, the BC is busy fixing problems and micromanaging, in part, to protect the kids from the stern GS. This marital combination snares children in an inescapable net of expectations and accountability. Nurturing has been lost, replaced by critique, consequences, and control, none of which solve the problems that created them. Coming from both parents, this firm-handed approach causes kids to feel collared, critiqued, and curtailed —and ultimately— less functional. Under these circumstances, it is easy to lose track of a child's heart.

Exchanges between these co-parents under pressure sound something like this:

GS: "Maya asked about a sleep-over Friday night. I said no, she had homework to do. She started crying, so I grounded her for the weekend."

BC: "You grounded her for crying?"

GS: "I grounded her for using high drama to dodge her homework again. Consequences will teach her a valuable lesson."

BC: "Well, she's struggling with science. I'll turn off the WiFi and make sure she reads her textbook. Please, don't raise your voice at her anymore tonight. I'll make sure things get done."

GS: "Do what you want. She has to improve her grades. And, I expect an apology."

In the scenario above, neither the GERMAN SHEPHERD nor the Border Collie will allow Maya to go to the sleep-over. The GERMAN SHEPHERD will be the first to implement the restriction, and the Border Collie will take over the management of the rule, essentially to protect the child from the GERMAN SHEPHERD parents' intense enforcement policy.

While the co-parenting relationship appears aligned and copacetic, the RIGHT & TIGHT partnership threatens to crush a child's spirit. Being over-managed, the child fails to develop their own sense of purpose, becomes anxious yet relies on what they resent most: parental control. A relationship containing both dependency and hostility emerges.

Another scenario with this parenting team is when parental expectations relentlessly drive children to strive. The steep gradient of success fatigues them. When children begin to falter due to the mounting pressure of both social functioning and performance expectations, it's time to seek help.

HOPE FOR THE STRESSED GERMAN SHEPHERD PARENT

Whether sad and lonely, angry and demanding, or merely disengaged from family actions, there is hope for the dependable **GERMAN SHEPHERD** parenting breed...and their family. For it must be said their family needs them. Their sense of duty and principle, their respect for virtues and traditions are essential ingredients for happy families, let alone civil societies.

But how to get back to the Green Zone so these wonderful attributes can be known? If you are co-parenting, read the section describing your partner's parenting style next. After that, skip ahead to Section III: The Three Stage Path to Harmony, for steps to healing your family.

Quick Quiz

A typical personal growth area for the GS Style is:

a. Dole out more advice and consequences to the kids

b. Relax expectations of others to enjoy the mild chaos of family life

c. Continue to ruminate about how right you are.

CHAPTER SIX

The Afghan Hound Parenting Style

"All you need is faith, trust, and a little bit of pixie dust."

PETER PAN

IF YOU'VE IDENTIFIED YOURSELF as an AFGHAN HOUND parent type, this chapter is for you! The AFGHAN HOUND is known as the "King of Dogs" due to its elegance and ability to track game over expansive terrain.

This breed, more curious than obedient, has an easygoing temperament and a preference for open spaces. How does this canine avatar translate to the bipedal parenting world?

LET'S TAKE A LOOK!

- - - - - - - - - - - - - - -

AT THEIR BEST, this parent is pleasant and engaging and blends spontaneity with playfulness to manage tasks.

AT THEIR WORST, this parent is inconsistent and reluctant regarding rules and expectations, avoids conflict while being superficially present, and can be sullen and self-absorbed.

DOMINANT BELIEFS: over time, most problems sort themselves out; children learn from their own mistakes.

LOVES TO: enjoy life and learn as you go.

CO-PARENTING: sniffs out the attentive BORDER COLLIE or compassionate GOLDEN RETRIEVER as romantic partners.

— — — — — — — — — — — —

Enthralled by novelty and relishing the spontaneous over the regimented, this parenting style's dog tag reads:

PARENTING STRENGTHS IN ACTION

"Huzzah!" to the **AFGHAN HOUND** parent, often described as the "nice" or "fun" parent. Don't be surprised to find an extrovert **AFGHAN HOUND** parent at the center of the neighborhood activities, attracting children from around the block for a pickup game of soccer or building a backyard tree house, or an introverted AH in the garage teaching a curious kid or two how to play the guitar. **AFGHAN HOUNDS** believes children will learn from their own successes and mistakes and that most problems, over time, will sort themselves out. Each little problem need not be dwelt upon; optimism rules the day. Besides, there are so many more enjoyable things to do other than focusing on the minutia of life's many problems.

Somebody toss that dog a chew toy!!

Could all this relaxed playfulness result in overlooking the mundane tasks involved in raising a family? Sure, but not to worry, there's always tomorrow…

With openness to life experiences and relative indifference to time-frames and deadlines, this parenting style seldom lands in research laboratories or accounting firms. Instead they are likely to wander down career paths of inventiveness and the arts, or sales and persuasion.

LOCATION ON THE MAP

Let's take a minute to appreciate the buoyant heart of the **AFGHAN HOUND** parenting style. The AH is found on the quadrant on the Map between ENCOURAGING & FLEXIBLE.

We begin with an in-depth look at the **AFGHAN HOUND** on the Nurture Scale. Nurture Scale = How this parent responds to a child's feelings. The AH is most at home on the ENCOURAGE end of the Nurture Scale.

To *encourage* is an act of optimism, a positive lean toward the future, sparking children's lives with knowledge and experiences. This fresh breath of optimism blows on embers of curiosity, helping children learn and grow. Discovery and learning occur naturally as children churn incremental failures into successes.

Kudos for easygoing encouragement in action!

AFGHAN HOUND and GERMAN SHEPHERD parent types both ENCOURAGE. The AFGHAN HOUND encourages spontaneity and relaxed engagement, while the GERMAN SHEPHERD encourages conventional wisdom and leadership.

Now, let's take a look at the **AFGHAN HOUND** parent type on the Structure Axis.

Structure Scale refers to the preferred manner of discipline, of teaching The 3Rs (Rules, Respect, and Responsibilities). The AH leans toward the FLEXIBLE end of the Structure Scale. FLEXIBLE: establishes routines by improvising and adjusting to the situation at hand.

The AH is more attentive to the *mood* of the family than formal rules and time-frames. Flexibility around rules and routines often leaves the AH improvising in the moment, with the likelihood of teaching children the same. With an eye toward pleasantries and adventure, and a disinclination toward the drudgery of daily life, many chores and duties are deferred until conditions announce these things *must* be done. Within a reasonably well-working family, this laidback approach responds to contingencies at hand, and the laundry gets done on the short cycle. Might this improvisational induce unease in co-parenting in the partner? We'll discuss this soon enough.

Keep in mind, this ENCOURAGE & FLEXIBLE parenting tendency falls on a continuum. The AH parent can firm up on household rules and will certainly comfort, but there will be a slight bias toward their natural style.

The AH's combined attributes of ENCOURAGE & FLEXIBLE inspire children toward exploration and adventure…though children may stray due to slack guidance.

Take a quick look at an AH parent handling a child who is running late for school.

THE AFGHAN HOUND, THE CHILD, AND THE SHOE

CHILD: "I can't find my other shoe! The bus is coming! Help me find my shoe!"

AH (picking up a pair of shoes from the pile at the front door): "Here, use these for today."

CHILD: "But those are my soccer shoes!"

AH (sipping coffee as a big yellow bus is seen pulling up)

"Gosh honey, suit yourself, the bus is here..."

CHILD: "*Aaaargh!* Okay, give me them!"

AH: " They look just fine. Don't worry.

The child runs to the bus in soccer shoes.

What's going on in this example? This parent, fairly oblivious to the child's distress, allows the child to feel natural consequences; such as feeling uncomfortable about her footwear or possibly being teased by peers. The child learns lessons and self-corrects as natural consequences motivate and shape behavior. In the days following, chances are this child will wake up on time and prepare responsibly.

ATTACHMENT THEORY AND THE AFGHAN HOUND PARENT

Attachment Theory is the psychological school of thought that shows how children flourish and develop through attuned and connected attachment with their caregivers.

Children benefit from caregivers who:

1. *Encourage* them to *explore*
2. *Support* them while they *persevere* through roadblocks in their exploration
3. *Comfort* them in order they may *recover* from fatigue and/or upset feelings

Congrats, AFGHAN HOUND! You ENCOURAGE children to explore, and SUPPORT them as they persevere in their efforts.

As you might guess, the **AFGHAN HOUND** parent is a natural when it comes to needed encouragement and support. The AH may be a bit under-responsive in comforting distressed children, but they are great at instigating joyful engagement with life.

Here's an example of an **AFGHAN HOUND** parent in action:

Young Henry sits on the back steps, bored.

AH: "Hey, Henry, let's shoot some hoops!"

HENRY: "Hmm, I don't know…"

AH (encourage): "Hey, I could use a shooting partner. My league plays this weekend, and I need to sharpen up."

The two of them go to the driveway to dribble and shoot. Pretty soon, neighborhood kids join. The AH parent pulls together a game while coaxing the kids on proper technique and good sportsmanship. The kids play while learning more about the game. Henry gets bumped and twists his ankle. He argues with the kid who bumped him, then seeks out his AH parent.

HENRY: "Max won't play fair! I don't want to play anymore."

AH: "Man, you guys play some tough ball. Why don't you and Max take a break and join us when you're ready."

HENRY: "I quit. My ankle hurts. I'm going to tell Mom since you don't care."

AH (support): "You bet. Have Mom take a look at that. Come back when you're ready to play again. We'll have a spot for you!"

Henry limps up the steps, watching the other kids return to the game. He really wants to rejoin his friends and wrestles with what to do next.

Well done, **AFGHAN HOUND** parent! Henry was encouraged to play and supported by this parent's buoyant cheerfulness. Though feeling a bit neglected about his injury, he considers rejoining the game; a sign of maturity! Regarding Henry needing comfort…well, this dog is dragging its tail.

THE AFGHAN HOUND'S PREFERRED METHOD OF GUIDING CHILDREN: FINESSE

Each of our four canine avatars has their own signature strategy of getting children to do what is expected of them. All parents use a variety of methods to guide and motivate children, but each parent pooch has their own distinct method, especially when stressed. Here are the four primary strategies: the principled **GERMAN SHEPHERD** enforces, the compassionate **GOLDEN RETRIEVER** persuades, the attentive **BORDER COLLIE** compels. And what about the easygoing **AFGHAN HOUND**? This parenting style's favored method is to finesse.

---

fi•nesse /fə'nes/ *verb*: to influence another person through in an artful manner absent of confrontation or conflict.

The three stages of *finesse*:

1. *Inducing* by using a compelling force of fun and optimism
2. *Convincing* by appealing to a sense of fairness or obligation
3. *Withdrawing* to allow natural consequences to shape behavior

Inducing refers to guiding children while using the AH's attractive lure of fun and optimism. Think of the entrancing powers of the Pied Piper and blend this with the child-like enthusiasm of Peter Pan. This is the **AFGHAN HOUND** style on a household scale. *Inducing* adds spice to the mundane and elicits cooperation, "Let's see who can clear the table the fastest!"

If that doesn't work, the second stage of finessing, *convincing*, is used. Convincing employs verbal prompting and appeals to fairness to gently prod children to get things done, "Haley, it's your turn to take out the garbage. Your brother did it last week."

And if that fails, the AH employs the third stage: *withdraw*. The AH has distaste for scolding, demanding, or applying consequences. When children refuse, resist, and avoid, this caregiver withdraws to the backyard, video screen, or gym; to let the situation sort itself out.

Here's a peek at how the AFGHAN HOUND'S easygoing finessing might sound in the family living room:

AH (inducing): "The piano recital is next week, Mr. Piano Man. You must be excited to show off your talent! Going to put some time in today?"

JAMAR: "Not now. I'm taking a break from practice. My friends need me online. We're in the middle of a video game."

AH (convincing): "I guess it's up to you. A lot of family and friends will be there. It's a good time to show your chops and feel proud of yourself."

JAMAR: "My friends are online *now*. Leave me alone! I'll do fine at the recital!"

AH (withdraw): "Hey, do as you want, dude. I just thought I would remind you."

In this scenario, the AH parent finesses the child toward responsible behavior. To keep the peace, the AH leaves the final decision to practice or play video games, to Jamar.

DIFFICULTIES FOR THE AFGHAN HOUND PARENT

For the AFGHAN HOUND parent's calm pleasantry and friendly engagement to work, a child must be receptive and willing—or at the very least neutral—about matters at hand. For example, a happy child needs little inducement from a parent to vacuum the living room. On the other hand, a sullen child is impervious to cheerful inducements. If a child's moodiness becomes chronic, the parent loses grip on the rope used to lasso the child's cooperation.

When the child's problems of heart are fairly obvious, as in the Green Zone, the AH might sort it out by drawing on their secondary strengths of *comfort* and *flexibility*.

If the AFGHAN HOUND fails in these efforts, however, they tend to give up and move to something more interesting and definitely less stressful. Sadly, it's this impulse that leaves the partner of an AFGHAN HOUND feeling unsupported and their children feeling disconnected.

CO-PARENTING AND THE AFGHAN HOUND PARENT

AFGHAN HOUNDS tend to co-parent alongside people opposite their ENCOURAGE orientation on the Nurture Scale, meaning they tend to pair up with a partner prone to COMFORT. The easygoing AFGHAN HOUND finds a BORDER COLLIE or GOLDEN RETRIEVER nearly irresistible. Conversely, the AFGHAN HOUND'S cool, laid-back manner charms the highly charged BORDER COLLIE and compassionate GOLDEN RETRIEVER type.

The AH parents are best when following the lead of their partner, enforcing the structure the other parent establishes, and ministering to the emotional needs of both partner and children. True, the AH may not feel completely comfortable with their partner's degree of structure, but the wise AH accepts the implicit wisdom of their partner's firmer approach to discipline and inclination toward a child's heart. Within this well-functioning partnership, love and trust are based upon the implicit understanding that the AFGHAN HOUND'S partner has deeper knowledge and wisdom about the details of family life that frankly aren't on the AH's radar screen. And of course, the co-parent/partner does well to recognize the tenderness at the center of the AH's buoyant heart.

Under sunny circumstances, when the AH's heart is inclined toward the hearts of their spouse and children, this parent generates joyful learning and adheres to routines of family life while transcending children's resistant behavior.

THE AFGHAN HOUND PARENT IN THE TURBULENT YELLOW AND RED ZONES

Goodness, what could go wrong with running a household in a laid-back manner? Well, the AHs reading this might say, "Yeah, what's wrong? We're chill!" Which is, of course, part of the problem. AHs tend to be a tad oblivious to the details and difficulties of family life.

In the Yellow Zone, the **AFGHAN HOUND**'s easy-going charm transforms into impatience and disengagement when family arguments become frequent or heated.

In the Red Zone, the **AFGHAN HOUND**'s impatience exacerbates problems.

This bon vivant parent type longs for positive emotions and disengages from conflict to seek small pleasures elsewhere. If cornered within the confines of inescapable parenting, a pattern of reactive anger and contrite retreat emerges as conflict does not suit the AH disposition.

THE FRUSTRATION/RESISTANCE CYCLE

In a classic physics experiment, striking one tuning fork will cause a neighboring tuning fork to resonate at the same frequency. Frustration/Resistance is the dynamic where a parent's visible frustration activates a child's resistance like two tuning forks resonating with each other. To understand its powerful influence over the emotions within the family, it deserves further exploration.

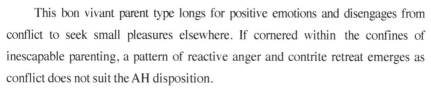

Intuitively, adults know a smile and rolling a ball toward a toddler will produce a smile and a ball rolled back. A parent's pleasant demeanor induces pleasant feelings in children. This cultivates a bloom of positive potential as children imitate, mimic, and cooperate with caregivers.

Less intuitive for caregivers is how an unpleasant parental interaction produces uncomfortable feelings in children. This spins a web of resistance toward their caregivers. When a parent uses an annoyed or irritable tone to send their child to bed, the child will undoubtedly whine and resist.

This hard-wired, psychosocial phenomenon exists within all social animals as they imitate, mimic, and attune to each other in a responsive, reflexive manner.

Frustration is the uncomfortable feeling that occurs when intentions are thwarted, and expectations aren't met. Each day, parents have numerous intentions and expectations. They *intend* to go to work, make nutritional meals, and raise good children. And, from dawn to dusk, they *expect* their kids to get up, get dressed, get out the door, do homework, and go to bed. When caregivers display frustration, the inevitable result is a child's resistance.

On a good day, a child may rise above their natural inclination to resist the demands of a frustrated adult and get ready before the bus comes. The parent may have banked enough goodwill to not trigger resistance, or, up to this point, the child has not had to endure multiple frustrations.

On a bad day, tolerance levels are depleted, and the child succumbs to the desire to resist— subconsciously landing a counter punch by stalling or arguing— and misses the bus.

In the Yellow and Red Zones, parental frustration and child resistance feed each other; spinning like a dog chasing its tail...and getting nowhere. This parent trap is called the Frustration/Resistance Cycle.

The troubled Yellow and Red Zones generate hungry hearts and hurt feelings. Children's upset emotions require comforting from caregivers. Unfortunately, the AFGHAN HOUND turns its tail to avoid sticky situations and bruised feelings and silently begs their partner to do the emotional heavy lifting.

In the language of Attachment Theory[3], this parenting type becomes "dismissive" of upset feelings experienced by those around them. Through instinctive imitation, children do the same. The AH resists negative family emotions and interactions. They ignore, deflect, and avoid.

The conflict-avoidant AFGHAN HOUND parent often reports feeling crowded out by negativity and what seems to them needless—and endless—conflict. Wishing to avoid the mayhem, the AH stays late at work, or escapes to the garage, or the gym, or immerses themselves in omnipresent media. The AH wishes to do anything to avoid discord—and on a deeper level—a sense of personal failure.

---

3 Mary Ainsworth: Parenting Styles

Let's take a look at the Frustration/Resistance Cycle spinning in the AH family room:

AH: "Hey, Frannie, time to go to hockey practice."

FRANNIE: "I don't want to go. I'm tired."

AH: "Aw, come on, last time was a lot of fun. You're the one that begged to play hockey."

FRANNIE: "I hate hockey. The coach never puts me in the game. I'm not going. I quit!"

AH: "You don't really mean that. Hey come on…your team is counting on you!"

FRANNIE: "I hate them! It's stupid!"

AH: "Your coach won't be happy. Well, Miss Debbie Downer, I'm going anyway."

In the above example, the child doesn't *intend* to be bratty, nor does the parent *intend* to abandon the family. Both are stuck in a cycle of parental frustration and child resistance. Parent and child are like tuning forks resonating with each other, but attuned in emotional distress. Of course, the AH parent only wants the child to participate in an activity that yields fun participation, but whatever distress the child is feeling is not being addressed. The parent initiates in good spirits, but in the end, the parent shows impatience that further fuels the child's resistance. Feelings of failure and resistance echo back and forth until the AH retreats to the rink to hang with the other parents. This is a classic Yellow Zone scenario for the AFGHAN HOUND parent.

What isn't explored is *why* the child is not willing to go to practice. The AH parent, often shying away from vulnerable emotions, doesn't ask, "What's wrong, honey? You have enjoyed the team practices before. Has something happened? I love you too much to make you do something you don't want to do."

Though missed by many stressed caregivers, developmentally speaking, children often don't know what emotion they are experiencing until an adult helps name these feelings with them.

The peace-seeking AH caregiver frequently gives up trying to finesse children into participating in activities or adhering to rules and responsibilities. In the Yellow or Red Zone, the AH retreats. Toxic resentment seeps into their heart, driving them further from the nuances of parenting and blinding them to the shadowland of the child's heart.

> When working with an AH parent in my clinical practice, I help deepen their capacity to feel, accept, and acknowledge their child's Three Vulnerable Emotions: sadness, loneliness, and fear.

In a Frustration/Resistance Cycle, the AH's wonderful gifts of adventurous learning and joyful living dissolve into a vague diminishment of participation.

As frustration and resistance continue between adults and children, it spreads and multiplies. Children begin to realize their dramatic protests, relentless complaining, and persistent avoidance work, so they do more of it. Sooner or later, the child becomes intuitively aware of exactly what it will take for the parent to give in. Each mirrors the other in a twisting, downward spiral of irritated demands and angry protests known as the Frustration/Resistance Cycle.

In the Green Zone, this type of interaction occurs occasionally, in the Yellow Zone, regularly, and in the Red Zone, frequently. When this prickly pattern begins to grow, it's time to reach for help.

CHILDREN OF THE STRESSED AFGHAN HOUND PARENT

When stressed, the easygoing **AFGHAN HOUND** blusters and barks but soon retreats to self-indulgence or something deemed more important. The child learns the AH parent has no wish for drawn-out battles and typically lacks follow-through, so may simply ignore the assigned task. And by fifth grade, most children —through intuition and trial and error—have learned which strategy works and with which parent. This, by the way, is evidence of emotional intelligence.

Kids lay siege against the AH parent, catapulting resistance against them until their thin wall of resolve crumbles.

Another method children use to neutralize the AH parent is to ramp up the emotional intensity of their protest, then down-shift to a softer plea. This often works on the AH, who mistakenly believes this "quieting" is the child's behavior being managed.

Dark implications arise for children if families operate in the troubled

Yellow and Red Zones for too long. Sure, children may avoid their responsibilities now and then. But in the long run, is this what they really need? Of course not. Parental disapproval and the child's failure to accomplish The 3Rs (Rules, Respect, and Responsibilities) diminishes the child's self-esteem and capacity to handle the myriad of tasks of childhood.

Of particular concern is the Afghan parent becoming cavalier about parenting or becoming "checked out," and leading children to feel insecure about the emotional distance of the parent.

> Processing emotions entails talking to an emotionally receptive adult about vulnerable feelings. Unable to process their vulnerable emotions, the child ultimately feels a bit less protected and a tad more troubled by the world.

Under this chaotic cloud, a child loses their connection to a calm and caring adult. The loss is twofold. First, there is a generalized disruption of emotional stability. Second, the child loses the ability to process emotions. Unable to fully share their intense feelings of frustration and anger—or their vulnerable feelings of sadness, loneliness, and fear—a silent ache forms in the child's heart.

The Big Three Vulnerable Emotions:
Sadness, Loneliness, Fear

Though desperate to connect with this parent, even young children will intuit the AH's limitation to handle stressful emotions and may act to protect this parent by hiding or disguising their own upset feelings.

Problems real and significant loom over families within the Yellow and Red Zones. The child knows they are loved but does not feel it. Their capacity to endure frustration shrinks, an ache for nurturing—a vague and nascent suffering—transmutes into diminished motivation and a compulsion to act out. Sibling cruelties, obnoxious behaviors, and backtalk erupt more frequently, sadly eroding the love once imagined of family life. Perplexed and dispirited, the AFGHAN HOUND parent is flummoxed about how to help the family.

In the turbulent home of a stressed **AFGHAN HOUND** parent, being emotionally removed has some obvious and glaring problems. The AH's shallow presence leaves a child seeking support and attention from the other parent, or if a single parent, the child is left to free range. This signals a cascade of problems awaiting the AH caregiver. The child's frustration and resistance deepens, and childrearing efforts are off-loaded onto the other parent, grandparents, teachers, or others... then what? There can be many variations to the scenario, but a checked-out **AFGHAN HOUND** often becomes sullen or retreats further into their own interests, appearing to family members as aloof, disengaged, or self-involved; leaving others feeling resentful.

There may be innumerable underlying reasons for a child's refusals and under-functioning. It's important to understand a child swims in a shadowland of invisible difficulties they can feel but often can't articulate.

Within this shadowland lies *situational* reasons for why a child may neglect responsibilities. Many reasons may not be apparent, such as needing additional time and emotional support to grieve the death of a pet, missing time with a parent who works late or who spends so much time with the new baby, or the echo of the word "divorce" overheard during his parent's heated argument the night before.

Equally important, there may also be personal reasons like ADHD, social anxiety, embarrassment over changing bodies, bullying, confusion about sex and gender identity, and the list is infinite. (And no, dear Yellow Zone **AFGHAN HOUND** parent, these are not just things kids will sort out as they go.)

Within a distressed family, frustration and anger echo back and forth between parent and child, and within a turbulent home, pain gathers in the hearts of children. Young children form habits of intense and obnoxious behaviors in order to garner parental attention and connection; innately, understanding negative attention is better than no attention at all. Older children will do the same to avoid the burden of responsibility. In both cases, insecurity bubbles in their guts, and children have no understanding of its origin.

To keep the emotional cauldron from boiling over in catastrophic intensity, distressed children develop very predictable strategies of resistance:

- Avoiding activities that normally would be enjoyable
- Blaming others for obvious self-failings
- Distracting themselves with media and devices to a harmful degree
- Fibbing in ways that seem senseless
- Instigating conflict with others to avoid feelings of failure

Though annoying, these defense mechanisms indicate the gripping stress that holds a child's tormented heart hostage.

> **Psychologically, a child with a heart wounded by sadness, loneliness, or fear has little recourse other than to resist the well-meaning expectations of others. To many caregivers, coaches, or teachers however, the child may simply appear irresponsible, immature, or poorly behaved.**

PARTNERS OF THE STRESSED AFGHAN HOUND

NURTURE

Regarding co-parenting relationships, predictable patterns and problems emerge for each parent type, especially under stress. Stress overwhelms parents, pushing them to the outer Yellow and Red Zones on the Map.

Remember, people choose partners opposite of themselves on the Nurture Scale. This means an **AFGHAN HOUND** tends to co-parent with a **Border Collie** or a **Golden Retriever**.

Sadly and predictably, the frustrated **AFGHAN HOUND** avoids and under-functions under stress, while a **Border Collie** partner becomes controlling, and a

Golden Retriever partner becomes overwhelmed.

In the Yellow and Red Zones, the AFGHAN HOUND and Border Collie pairing becomes the GOOD COP/BAD COP couple. The AFGHAN HOUND and the Golden Retriever become the LOOSEY-GOOSEY couple.

Let's take a look at each parenting team under stress.

In a GOOD COP/BAD COP pairing, the conflict-averse "Good Cop" AFGHAN HOUND and the enforcer "Bad Cop" Border Collie square off. The power struggles between the Border Collie parents and children generate emotional heat and turmoil. The AFGHAN HOUND, inclined to engage with sunny emotions and avoid stormy ones, retreats into their own world.

Whether it's work, hobbies, or something else, the AH seeks some modicum of positive engagement outside of the family. The predictable marital result? The BC fumes about feeling abandoned. The AH retreats further. The BC amps up, and the AH retreats further still. Before long, anxiety, resentment, and stress have everybody reeling.

The GOOD COP/BAD COP relationship ends up sounding something like this:

AH: "I gave Brittany permission to go to a party tonight."

BC: "What? She's behind on homework. Yesterday she told me to shut up and I grounded her for it. She knows she's grounded. She's playing us off each other. You have to check with me before you start handing out permission. You have no idea what's going on around here!"

AH: "Hey, all she wants to do is get out of the house and have fun like a normal kid. It's not like she's failing fourth grade, you know. She wanted to tell you, but she was afraid you'd throw a fit."

BC: "Seriously? Why do I always have to be the bad guy while you do as you damn well please, undermining me and going behind my back? You let her have her way so she'll like you. Well, that's being a friend, not a parent!"

AH: "Wow, no wonder Brittany wants to get away from you. You're so damned controlling nobody wants to be around you. You and Brittany go ahead and keep yelling at each other! I'll be cleaning the gutters."

The intense dialog dramatized above might seem trivial, but interactions like these leave emotional scars.

The other common pairing is the AFGHAN HOUND & Golden Retriever pairing, which I call the LOOSEY-GOOSEY couple. Both caregivers are lax with family structure, and both tend to be conflict-avoidant. A hallmark of this union is children who nip and bite at the hand that feeds them by ignoring rules or over-riding parental resolve with dramatic outbursts.

As far as family life goes, these partnerships become stressed and polarized. The AFGHAN HOUND parent, once full of spontaneous optimism, now struggles to sustain resolve when it comes to rules and routines, while the Golden Retriever partner attempts to sustain structure with melodramatic flare-ups:

Here's an example of a LOOSEY-GOOSEY couple trying to accomplish some morning planning:

AH: "Maddy says she's going to a matinee and wants some money, but you won't give her any…you just yell at her."

GR: "I gave her money yesterday, and now she wants more? I suppose she was crying and telling you how mean I am. I do everything around here, and she never lifts a finger to help."

AH: "Well, what should I do? Should I tell her she can't go?"

GR: "What good will that do? She'll just find a way to do what she wants anyway. Why don't you just come home from work on time and cook dinner for once? It's not fair I end up doing all the cooking. We both work full-time."

AH: "Okay, okay, okay. I'll take care of Maddy. You go ahead and go to work. I'll see you later tonight with Chinese take-out."

GR: "You don't get it. You just don't get it!!"

AH strides upstairs to scold Maddy…then gives her twenty dollars.

During workshops, I've asked, "To those of you married to an AFGHAN HOUND parent, what might you expect of children being raised primarily by the AFGHAN HOUND parent type?"

Answers instantly ring out, "Children go to school wearing pajamas!" "Kids falling asleep in front of the TV!"

Within these bemused answers, there seems to be an implied fear that, left alone with the AFGHAN HOUND caregiver, children will devolve into a Lord of the Flies environment where, in short order, kids will don war paint and hunt their siblings with sharpened broom handles.

These classic co-parenting complaints stem from a belief the AH is not competent—or does not care enough to become competent—when it comes to structure and discipline.

From the **AFGHAN HOUND'S** point of view comes the complaint they feel mired in the minutia of unnecessary conflict. When I shared this thought during a workshop, a woman blurted out, "You make it sound like I should feel sorry for him. He's at home sorting fishing lures while I'm here at this workshop. No offense, but as usual, I'm doing all the work!" This **Border Collie** parent is expressing two common complaints about being married to an **AFGHAN HOUND**: feeling neglected by their spouse, and feeling overwhelmed by the seemingly sole burden of childrearing. The **AFGHAN HOUND'S** disengagement leaves their mate feeling like a single parent, or worse, undermined in their effort to parent effectively. This lack of support from their partner brews a potent poison for any partnership: resentment.

This is reflected in a common refrain heard from **Border Collie** partners that sounds something like this, "I have three children: one in third grade, one in sixth grade, and my spouse makes three." Being viewed as another child by their spouse is not conducive to pleasant conversation… or a happy sex life.

HOPE FOR THE STRESSED AFGHAN HOUND PARENT

Whether distracted, avoidant, or merely superficially involved with family details, there is hope for the easy-going **AFGHAN HOUND** parenting breed… and the family. For it must be said that their family needs them. Their lighthearted and laid-back demeanor, their love of creativity and discovery, are critical ingredients for happy families, let alone inspired societies.

Ahead are strategies to map your return to the Green Zone where this parent's wonderful attributes will shine. But first, if you are co-parenting, read the section describing your partner's parenting style. After that, skip ahead to **Section III: The Three Stage Path to Harmony** for steps to healing your family.

Quick Quiz

A typical personal growth area for the Afghan Hound Style is:

a. Grab some "me time" at a local golf course.

b. Use sticky notes to remind your partner, "Don't worry! Be happy!"

c. Begin listening for hurt feelings in family members and be more curious about their issues at hand.

FAMILY THERAPY SOLUTIONS

CHAPTER SEVEN

The Three-Stage Path to Harmony
Awareness, Quieting, Awakening

STAGE ONE: AWARENESS: GENERATING UNDERSTANDING, ACCEPTANCE, AND STRATEGIC THINKING

Awareness is critical to all endeavors of the mind. Awareness generates intention, stirs motivation, sharpens focus, and invites strategic course corrections.

Good news! By determining your parent pooch on the Map, you are already well along the path of *awareness*. Learning the strengths and weaknesses of your main parenting style brought self-awareness—and hopefully—respect for other styles of parenting.

In the previous chapters, you put a pin on the Map indicating your Family Stress Zone and the best path needed to return the family to balance and harmony.

The sections on co-parenting confirmed the universal notion that "opposites attract" and revealed the predictable *patterns* of conflict that arise when stress further polarizes couples.

Finally, awareness expanded further with the knowledge that getting trapped in a Frustration/Resistance Cycle insidiously drives families into the turbulent Yellow and Red Zones on the Map.

Equipped with a new understanding of family dynamics and principles, your heart has become a compass on the journey toward harmony. Well done!

*Using visual representations, the Map
enables people to use their intuitive wisdom
to problems at hand.*

By now, you have likely applied the Map's parenting model to a broader context of your life. Most people end up plotting their partners, parents, in-laws, and even teachers and coaches on the Map, now thinking of them in terms of the four dog breed parenting styles and pondering the effect on their child's personal development.

Now, let's continue the journey to family harmony. Though rigorous—because all change is difficult—these next stages are satisfying and often exhilarating as children trend toward cooperation and happiness. The process of Awareness, Quieting, and Awakening has been used in my clinical practice for over two decades. In the chapters ahead, you'll read about others who have walked *The Three Stage Path to Harmony*.

So now we turn to Quieting and Awakening. These are essential stages to unleashing your parenting potential. These stages are sequential. You'll need to accomplish a few simple outcomes in Stage Two: Quieting, before moving on to the final stage, Awakening.

STAGE TWO: QUIETING: CREATING CALM BY MANAGING YOUR EMOTIONS

The Quieting stage places emphasis on managing your upset emotions better. This stage of the journey involves mindfulness and emotional self-regulation, or as a **GERMAN SHEPHERD** Parent at a workshop wryly stated, "Sounds like you're saying I should stop yelling at the kids."

To which I replied, "Exactly."

When caregivers *quiet* (by controlling their emotions and reducing expressed anger and frustration toward children), children respond in kind by *quieting* their reflexive resistance, which includes backtalk, tantrums, and meltdowns. As an added bonus, caregivers are more likely to enjoy—and be able to influence—their children.

You're probably thinking, "Easier said than done." Caregivers will inevitably blow it now and then and show frustration and anger toward children. But, thankfully, clinical experience shows this only becomes a problem when expressed parental anger exceeds a few times a month or when amends are not made after such episodes. When emotions go unchecked and unaddressed too long, the Frustration/Resistance Cycle starts spinning, gains momentum, and spreads unhappiness throughout the family.

> The importance of making amends: When a parent doesn't own, explain, and offer an apology for yelling at a child, the child has little recourse but to assign their own meaning to the incident such as labelling themselves as defective or unlovable, blaming others, or projecting lasting resentment onto the parent.

Despite the fact people don't like being angry, frustration and anger are quite commonplace in the home. Many of us were raised in families that yelled, criticized, or blamed. In essence, we were taught to parent using those counter-productive methods. When fatigued from the complexities of life and family, we may slip into a default mode of frustration and anger.

Additionally, more than a few parents have difficulty managing anger due to troubled childhoods and traumatic events of their past, and become triggered by family strife.

To make matters more difficult, many children have physical, mental, or emotional complications that can drive even the most skilled parent into therapy.

And if that weren't enough, there are social media and technology which, left unchecked, hold children and parents hostage with its addictive powers. This relatively new and devastating phenomenon is one our culture has not yet learned to manage. No wonder thorny interactions emerge in the landscape of parenting!

There are many reasons anger and frustration become a problem. But the answer is clear: caregivers must decrease expressions of anger and frustration (self-regulate emotions) if parent/child interactions are to improve.

This essential truth is embedded in our evolutionary ancestry and neurobiology: When a primate ancestor on the African veldt spied fruit in a bush, her excited, emotional system kicked out norepinephrine, fueling the furry biped to scamper for a fistful of berries.

Should the simian spy a circling pack of hyaenas, however, her emotional system sends her scrambling swiftly up a tree and out of harm's way. She will remain there, wary and resisting any urge to return to the ground, until the growling threat has retreated.

The neurological purpose of emotions is to activate us to *approach* situations that contribute to our well-being and *avoid and resist* situations that present potential harm. So when caregivers express frustration and anger toward children, they become the monkey equivalence of hyaenas, ceasing to be a nurturing presence and instead activating resistance from children.

When a family is functioning in the Green Zone, most children can endure an episodic outburst from their caregivers, knowing love and care are just around the corner.

And if they've misbehaved, children sense issues will be resolved with kind understanding.

In the Yellow and Red Zones, however, children's emotional reserves are depleted, and a primitive response of *resist* or *avoid* prevails.

As you reduce expressed frustration and anger, expect to wait two to three weeks before noticing behavior improvements, as children cling to the control and familiarity felt within the Frustration/Resistance Cycle. Additionally, the child's behavior may escalate at times as they fall back on tried and true behavior patterns used to deflect and distract the parent.

Where you lead, children will follow.
Replace frustration and anger with patience
and kindness

STAGE THREE: AWAKENING: EMPATHETIC ENGAGEMENT WITH CHILDREN

During the previous stage, Quieting, your family's Frustration/ Resistance Cycle will have slowed enough for both parent *and* child to notice. Now it's time to begin the journey to *Awakening*, with Stage III Parenting Tip Cards to guide you on the road to harmony.

In this stage, you'll begin to deepen your parental influence.

Awakening strategies activate a child's innate motivation to cooperate and achieve

---

These strategies and tips will elevate your childrearing skills to the realm of therapeutics. Besides having a guiding and corrective influence on children, you will learn how to have a healing effect, as well.

To produce this profound effect, we'll *awaken* the attachment system between parent and child, as in all warm-blooded animals. The attachment system creates a web of yearning and satisfaction between parents and children. Also known as the caregiving system,[4] attachment originates deep in the brain of both parents and children. They lie in tandem with other basic and compelling drives, such as thirst and hunger. In daily life, attachment between child and parent occurs naturally through breastfeeding, playing, cuddling, grooming, fixing boo-boos, and quiet conversations at bedtime. This nurturing intimacy powerfully and positively shapes the child's psyche toward the parent.

Once again, these truths of developmental growth stem from our mammalian history and discoveries in the field of neurobiology.

In the 1960s, psychiatrist and researcher John Bowlby studied the powerful phenomenon of attachment within primate groups.[5] Within troops of chimpanzees, he discovered mothers and their pups were bound by an elastic relationship of caregiving, where pups explore the environment and return to

---

[4] *The Archaeology of Mind: Neuro-evolutionary Origins of Human Emotion.* Panksepp, J., and Biven, L. (2012). New York: W. W. Norton & Company.

[5] *A Secure Base: Parent-Child Attachment and Healthy Human Development.* John Bowlby (1988) Basic Books of the Perseus Books Group.

their mother for nurturing and protection. Mothers and pups are seemingly attached by a magnetic field of mutual attraction. Neuroscientist Dr. Jaak Panksepp, a pioneer in the field of affective neurobiology, formally described this as "the care-giving motivational system within the adult, and reciprocating panic/grief system in the young."[6]

Fostering a protective orbit of nurture and structure, the mother chimp allows her young to explore the forest vicinity within range of sight, scent, and vocalization. When the pups become fatigued and hungry, they return to their mother to rest and recover, or cry in distress to signal for help.

For humans, so vulnerable and helpless at birth and through many years of maturing, the attachment period is long and complex. Each stage of development scaffolds on top of the previous: from infancy, where the nervous system facilitates the ability to feed and smile, to toddlerhood, in which language acquisition emerges, to grade school, where reading and writing and friendships are formed and forged. By the teen years, the attachment strands, though still present, shift toward self-sufficiency, peer relationships, and other caring adults within a young person's social sphere.

When the strands of attachment stretch and strain, a child feels distressed. Separated from the mother, an eighteen-month-old will cry in protest. A toddler, noticing mom walking into the next room, may whimper. Dropping off a youngster at a new daycare requires the masterful misdirection of a magician to slip unseen out the door. The first days of kindergarten, first sleepovers, and overnight camps, all strain and stretch the strands of attachment through the normative stress of growth and development.

Within families in the troubled Yellow and Red Zones, the stiff demands of raising children combine with a ratcheting turn of the Frustration/Resistance Cycle. Attachment strands between child and caregiver begin to fray. Rising from an ineffable ache for attachment, children develop a thirst for connections that compel, distract, and compromise. The drive for attachment *compels* children to seek attention using negative behaviors like picking on siblings seen as competition for parental attention. It *distracts* children from taking on challenges or shutting down their brain-numbing devices, tragically making them hesitant to explore the greater world. And it *compromises* their ability to endure frustration and solve problems.

---

[6] *The Archaeology of Mind: Neuro-evolutionary Origins of Human Emotion.* Panksepp, J., and Biven, L. (2012). New York: W. W. Norton & Company.

Essentially, children quench their thirst on the contaminated water of negative attention and the saccharine elixir of screen time, unsure when the next drink of a caregiver's nurturing nectar will come.

The awakening strategies ahead are designed to provide a healthy drink for a child's thirsty heart. Relief and trust develop, and peace of mind emerges. Through repeated and consistent application of these strategies, children are shaped toward the wishes of caregivers. A mutual relationship of reciprocal cooperation and respect begins to grow and blossom.

Proceed to the following chapters to read clinical stories of each parenting breed in therapy, and learn how parents like you begin to awaken to a more influential and therapeutic way of parenting.

Enjoy this front-row seat as families make their way along *The Three Stage Path To Harmony.*

CHAPTER EIGHT

The Golden Retriever Parent in Family Therapy

SEVERAL MONTHS AGO, a woman named Angela came to my office for help. She had been to one of my workshops and identified her parenting style as a GOLDEN RETRIEVER. A single mom, Angela separated from her husband, who had become addicted to opioids after back surgery and had slumped into a deep depression. Angela's two children, Owen, age twelve, and his sister Amanda, a year older, frequently fought.

"If I'm not there to constantly supervise, Amanda torments her brother." She continued sadly, saying she thought she had failed her family.

As a nurse supervisor at a local hospital, Angela's two children attend an after-school program. "I pick them up and by the time we get home, I've had it already with their yelling and fighting," she said. "They're cruel to each other."

Angela dropped her head in her hands and sighed, "This shouldn't be happening in our family. We love each other, but something's terribly wrong."

STAGE ONE: AWARENESS

I placed the Map in front of Angela. I guided her in discovering her place on the Nurture and Structure Scales leading to the GOLDEN RETRIEVER parenting style on the Map, "Yep, that's me: GOLDEN RETRIEVER."

Next, I gave her a GOLDEN RETRIEVER Parenting Card describing the GOLDEN RETRIEVER type.

THE GOLDEN RETRIEVER

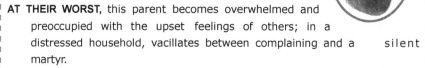

AT THEIR BEST, this parent patiently and compassionately provides emotional warmth and kindness to others and gracefully guides and cajoles children through daily routines and responsibilities.

AT THEIR WORST, this parent becomes overwhelmed and preoccupied with the upset feelings of others; in a distressed household, vacillates between complaining and a silent martyr.

DOMINANT BELIEFS: Love will conquer all. Be nice to others, and they will be nice in return.

LOVES to love and be loved.

CO-PARENTING: sniffs out principled GERMAN SHEPHERDS or easygoing AFGHAN HOUNDS.

THE GENTLE GOLDEN RETRIEVER parent style nurtures the hearts and minds of children, but the heart comes first. Therefore their dog tags read:

She nodded, "That's me! Especially the part about being easily manipulated."

Her friends tell her she's too accommodating, and she admits to being prone to playing the victim.

Moving next to The Family Stress Test, Angela scored her family in the Yellow Zone. The key indicators for Yellow Zone placement include the frequency of sibling fighting, Owen's emerging problems with peer relationships, and attention-seeking classroom behaviors. I asked Angela if the Yellow Zone seemed accurate to her. She nodded, saying their family wasn't quite in the Red Zone, "We can still have fun together but it's not easy."

While obviously optimistic, Angela described herself as an overwhelmed GR. Angela clearly wished she had help with all the logistics of raising a family.

During this session, Angela became aware of her parenting inconsistencies and her tendency to become dramatic when things got stressful. But she added hopefully, "At least things don't feel completely out of control."

I could see why Angela was a good RN. She easily diagnosed her family situation. She could also see a path leading to the healthy Green Zone, "I need to guide myself to the center of the Map and not get so worked up and dramatic… especially in the morning when everyone is under pressure to get out the door on time."

Angela and I were on the same page. "Between now and our next appointment," I asked, "what would you like to do differently?"

Angela listed a whole host of things she wanted to try, "Stop yelling. Be more positive... be more grateful. And, add more structure...especially around homework getting done."

I told Angela how much I appreciated her dedication to hard work and her willingness to jump directly into the deep end. She was eager to make changes fast, but suggested we pick one thing to focus on. Success with a single thread of life teaches us a lot more than pulling on a lot of strings all at once.

STAGE TWO: QUIETING: CREATING CALM BY MANAGING YOUR EMOTIONS

To address Angela's goals to be more positive and to stop yelling, I defined the concept of *quieting*. She must reduce not only yelling but *all* negative tones, nagging, and any unpleasant form of communicating. I recommended she focus on maintaining a sense of personal calm with morning routines.

I handed her the parenting card: "Reset Button for AM Routines," and advised her to give a couple of reminders to the kids, and then let the chips fall where they may.

Reset Button for AM Routines

A. Apologize for nagging your child to get up

B. Empathize with how the child must feel to be nagged in the morning.

C. Encourage and promote (I'll be more pleasant and you decide if you want to be on time!)

D. Allow natural consequences with empathy

EXAMPLE:

I am so sorry for nagging you to get up in the morning. It must put you in a bad mood, and I don't want to do that. From now on, I'm working on not nagging. We'll just get ready for school and wait for you in the car until your ready. I sure am proud to have a son like you. We can do this."

Next day: *The child gets into the car late and is angry.* "It's okay if we are a little late. I'm proud that you made it." The child will handle being late with his teacher.

"If they are late for school, that's fine. If you have to call in their dad or grandparent to bring them in, that's fine. If they yell at you for making them late, that's fine."

As a therapy team, Angela and I were working toward a happier family. I assured her that her children would slowly adjust to the new normal, her unfamiliar calm, and the gentle nudge of natural consequences.

> Morning school routines are a good place for parent's to conduct "worthy experiments" for change within the family. Children have a built in motivation to get to school on time, though they may test limits a few times.

TWO WEEKS LATER:

Angela arrived at our appointment reporting the kids had been late for school a couple days and blamed her for it, but overall, mornings were improving.

"I'll keep doing what I'm doing there," she said. "What I really need help with now is how to keep the peace after school."

"Let me tell you something you already intuitively know," I said with a smile. I told her she had already made a lot of progress by discovering her parenting style (her strengths and weaknesses) and her family's Stress Zone. She had purposefully made changes in her own behavior by being less dramatic, and her children responded by being more cooperative. All good signs.

Angela's eagerness to move on to another problem area was a great indicator of her willingness to make changes. I recommended she hold steady with her new morning approach, however, and let things settle into the habit. The quick progress made on morning routines showed just how influential Angela could be.

At this visit, I addressed the prospect that Angela's kids were experiencing emotional distress due to the separation.

"Emotional distress," I explained, "nudges families into the Yellow Zone." I asked if her children were showing any signs of emotional distress.

"It's pretty obvious," she admitted. "Owen cries at bedtime and asks when his dad is coming home."

Angela's daughter, Amanda, refuses to talk about it. Also, Angela could tell each child was demanding more attention from her. "I don't know how I could be with them more than I am," she said. "Besides work and school, I'm always with them."

Angela's own heart was hurting over her children's struggle and broken hearts.

When I acknowledged Angela's pain, she hid her face in her hands and cried.

I expressed how proud I was of her being willing to feel so deeply about her situation. Crying honors the heart and permits some sadness to melt away. "You are creating meaning out of a deep ache." I could see the relief on her face.

After a few minutes, she was ready to attack the problem with my guidance. "What can I do," asked Angela, "about their broken hearts?"

STAGE THREE: AWAKENING: EMPATHIC ENGAGEMENT WITH CHILDREN

"Here's what you can do," I began, "you can increase the nurturing they feel from you." I'm addressing the *quality* of the nurturing Angela gives her children. High-quality nurturing is easily swallowed and digested.

"This is a good and kind thing to do," I assured her. "This will calm them." And I gave her the good news, "**GOLDEN RETRIEVERS** are made for this kind of thing! You'll do great."

Angela was intrigued and leaned forward for the recipe to the secret sauce I was about to divulge. She had already given me clues as to where to start.

"You mentioned Owen seems sad about his dad and is weepy at bedtime," I said. She nodded and explained that Owen comes to her room at bedtime to talk. She tries her hardest to explain things and cheer him up, but they usually end up arguing, and he calls her names. Half the time, he falls asleep in her bed; emotionally spent.

"Angela, are you able to hear from Owen how sad and scared he is about his life right now, or would it overwhelm you?"

There is a deep inhale, then Angela says, "Frankly, I'm a little scared to hear about it; but I will, if it will help him. It just breaks my heart to see how sad he is."

This is great news. Angela was willing to do the tough job of looking deeper into her child's broken heart. To do this, she must help him *process* his emotions. This entails addressing *The Three Vulnerable Emotions: sadness, loneliness, and fear*.

"In the next few nights, snuggle with Owen and ask him about his sad, or lonely, or scared feelings, whichever you sense is on his mind." I continued, "Just listen. Allow him to share his big feelings, like you did with me today." I told her to invite him to share his sadness, loneliness, or fear, using a warm and gentle voice in order to give him relief, the same kind of relief Angela experienced when she cried in my office.

With her own tears, Angela recognized her heart's pain, honored the sadness in her life, made sense of her inner ache, and began to transcend the hurt.

Now she could give that gift of healing to Owen.

I handed her the Empathetic Listening Parenting Tip Card.

Empathic Listening
Reduce negative emotions and promote understanding by reflecting how a child might be feeling.

EXAMPLES

You seem..............*MAD... SAD...*
You sound............*HAPPY... NERVOUS...*
You look...............*FRUSTRATED*
I wonder if you are... *WORRIED*

Do: convey warmth, and let your child do the talking.
Don't : critique or advise.

Guiding children (anyone, actually) toward melting their sadness means helping them process emotions around worry or concern. Processing is done using empathic listening. Empathetic listening means listening closely with a sympathetic voice, kind eyes, and being as physically close to the person as is comfortable for them. This forms a safe, emotional cocoon around the child, allowing the child's feelings to surface. Feeling support, the child will typically begin talking about what's troubling him. The result is a shared understanding between parent and child. An emotional state of attuned, elastic intimacy forms between parent and child; a bond of loyalty and trust.

Within this sympathetic space, the child's self-defense mechanism drops as the parent *names*—and helps the child *know*—his vulnerable, uncomfortable feelings.

Under these secure conditions, a child may emote their feelings through tears. The caregiver can support emotional processing with phrases like, "I'm so proud of you, sweetheart for allowing yourself to feel such big feelings," or "I'm so sorry this feels so big," or "We'll get through this together."

Angela continued this healing work with her children. Both children, within the compassionate cocoon of their mother's love, talked and felt through their grief and concerns about their dad and their family's new situation. As feelings were processed, understanding grew, and she and her children shared thoughts and feelings openly and constructively.

Emotions are processed when thoughts and feelings are shared with a kind and patient listener.

In time, I met both of Angela's children in their venerable journey toward patience, love, and kindness to each other. Owen and Amanda sat on the couch, rambling on excitedly about their fairy garden where they hid trinkets and treasures for neighbor kids to find. It was obvious their mother's compassion and influence had shaped them. With Angela's dedication, the family crossed happily into the Green Zone.

POSTSCRIPT:

A few months later, I met their father, Patrick. He was a proud man with a wounded heart and the twinkling eyes of a feisty Irishman. Those eyes of greenish-blue reminded me of my deceased father, also a man of Irish descent. My pause was broken by Patrick asking if I was okay, "You look like you've seen a ghost."

I stammered, "Goodness, Patrick, I had a flashback of my father."

As we continued in conversation, Patrick paused to ask if I liked my dad. When I was a child, during his drinking years, I developed an ache for my father as alcohol dissolved the many wonderful things I wanted from him. And later, I hated him—but really it was just sadness— sadness that in this brief life, so much was lost. But toward the end of his life, and for many years, we loved each other radiantly through and through, like the sun on water.

Patrick nodded as we both sat; the room humming from the fan in my office window.

"Well," I smiled, "maybe we'll talk about that another time. For right now, tell me, how's your day going? I've met your family, and it seems you're a man of many blessings."

CHAPTER NINE

The Border Collie Parent in Family Therapy

YEARS AGO, Jessica, a no-nonsense twenty-something, escaped a hardscrabble life in a taconite mining town. When she moved to the Twin Cities, Jessica worked with me regarding her goals around anger and substance abuse. Since then, she'd established a satisfying career as an office manager for the county.

Now years later, I heard from Jessica again. As a single mom, Jessica worried about the growing conflict between her and her daughter Ruthie, age eleven.

I was pleased to see Jessica looking healthy and professional. With some history and trust already established, I jumped right in, "So you mentioned Ruthie is not getting up on her own for school. That's got to be frustrating."

"I need to do something," she said, plopping into her usual seat.

Jessica described their mornings as something that starts out pleasant, "I open her door and say, 'G'morning Sunshine,' then maybe sing the sunshine song." That hardly ever rouses Ruthie, she admitted, so she returns minutes later to flick the lights and remind her in a louder voice.

"Is that when she cheerfully hops out of bed and thanks you for being so supportive of her education and future?" I grinned.

"Yeah, no, she doesn't thank me," she laughed. Ruthie was, in fact, rude and sulking at breakfast.

"So what happens," I asked, "on the days when reminders and flicking the lights don't work?"

"I keep a bag of marbles in the freezer and pour them between her sheets," she explained. "The marbles roll wherever she rolls in the bed...works every time." She glanced down sheepishly.

"And that's when she thanks you for being so supportive...?"

Of course, I fully deserved a kick in the shin, but Jessica needed to hear how her efforts, though well-meaning, weren't going to achieve the results she was after. I offered Jessica a spot at one of my workshops for parents just like her.

AWARENESS, QUIETING AND AWAKENING... IN ONE SESSION

A week later, I got an email from Jessica, "I'm sorry I had to duck out of the workshop early. Ruthie cracked her head open, jumping around like a goofball, and I had to take her to Urgent Care." Her email said she'd been at the workshop long enough to determine her parenting style. "You probably already figured this out, but I'm a BORDER COLLIE!" Jessica admitted she had always used a "tough love" approach and liked running a "tight ship." (Awareness)

THE BORDER COLLIE

AT THEIR BEST, this parent attends to family life with vigilance and diligence and is unflagging while resolving problems.

AT THEIR WORST, this parent tends to micromanage and engage in power struggles and has fears of catastrophic outcomes

DOMINANT BELIEF: if I don't do it...it won't get done.

LOVES to be involved and assist others when help is needed.

CO-PARENTING typically chooses a companion more relaxed about the daily details of family life: the AFGHAN HOUND or GERMAN SHEPHERD.

With perked ears, busily directing and herding children, this parenting style's dog tag reads: ATTENTIVE !

Putting Ruthie to bed that night after the visit to Urgent Care, Jessica was tempted to remind Ruthie of the importance of being more careful next time and explain the financial cost of a hospital visit. "Instead, I decided to comfort her rather than correct her," Jessica wrote. (Quieting)

Jessica told Ruthie how much she loved her and how scared she was when she heard Ruthie was hurt. "I made my voice gentle and warm like you suggested."

Ruthie cried for twenty minutes, Jessica continued, telling her mom she felt like nobody loved her. Jessica cried too, and said she could relate to how Ruthie felt, but hadn't realized till then that Ruthie felt the same way. "I felt no one loved me my whole life!" (Awakening) Jessica ended her missive, saying, "I don't know why this worked, but I do know she got up on time the next morning and said 'thanks' when I poured her some orange juice! Something was different...*better*."

It was a giant step in the right direction. Jessica used the Map to guide her words and steer their relationship toward more tranquil seas. Aware of her parenting style, Jessica learned to ignore her instinct to micromanage, as a stressed BORDER COLLIE is prone to do. Jessica also found *quieting with compassion* was the kinder and more effective course of action and talked to Ruthie in a soft, loving tone. She was now able to reach deep into the hurting heart of a little girl who didn't have the happiness of one who bounds out of bed in the morning. Jessica fed her daughter compassion, and Ruthie sobbed; devouring every morsel of her mother's nurturing expressions of love.

This quick success, though a blessing to each of them, is unusual. My clinical experience shows parents must *quiet* for two to three weeks before they see a decrease in a child's resistance. Typically, behavior issues get worse before they get better as children test a parent's resolve. As mentioned in early chapters, emotions are like tuning forks. As the parent tuning fork vibrates in on a positive note, so too will the child tuning fork vibrate harmoniously...*at a point soon to come*.

As with learning anything, of course, this new strategy of quieting will fade if not practiced routinely. Situational or relational stress may fog our minds and leave us wallowing in the same old ways.

After a few weeks, Jessica returned to my office, "Tell me how to do this quieting thing again, and why? Ruthie is being a total brat, and she's driving me nuts!" Jessica appeared resentful, as if all this gentle kindness simply gave Ruthie the upper hand.

I handed Jessica a Frustration/Resistance Parenting Tip Card. "Put this on the fridge," I told her. "I'll toss in a magnet as a bonus."

"*Ooooh*," she said with a sarcastic smile. "Very generous, Doc."

I introduced the Frustration/Resistance concept to Jessica.

"Your frustration," I explained, "fuels Ruthie's resistance. Stop showing her your frustration. Replace your negative tones with pleasant ones. Fewer commands, more inviting requests, and her naughtiness will fade. In other words, you lead; she will follow."

SLOW THE SPIN!! of the Frustration / Resistance Cycle

Reduce expressions of frustration by reducing YOUR nagging, scolding, arguing, critiquing.

Be patient. Allow natural consequences and other influences to take effect.

"Do I tell her I'm turning over a new leaf or keep it a secret?" Jessica asked. "I'm afraid if I don't show her who's boss, she'll take advantage of the situation and act even worse."

I asked Jessica to consider how she would have felt if her mother had talked to her in a gentle and soft voice? Or told her how happy she was to be the mother of such a smart little girl? Or sat on the sofa with her to watch a movie?

"It might not be successful every time you need her to do something," I cautioned, "but this approach has the best track record of success...over time."

Jessica's childhood was filled with adversity due to her mother's abuse and drug use, making it hard for her to even imagine a kind and stable home setting.

Jessica grew up wary, overly protective, and preoccupied with managing others under her roof. She existed in survival mode.

"If your mom had been able to provide a stable, loving home," I told her, "you would have been more cooperative and accepting of her guidance."

Jessica nodded wistfully, "I'll work on showing Ruthie more compassion."

Over the coming weeks, Ruthie continued to shape toward Jessica's compassion and acceptance.

They came to my office a few times per year. There was a common refrain: I would ask Ruthie how she wanted to be parented around any one issue. Ruthie would voice a reasonable idea, and I would ask Jessica if she could live with that. Jessica always said with a sly smile, "Barely."

I suggested Jessica follow Ruthie's ideas as a worthy experiment, "Ruthie gets to learn from her own mistakes, and there's the added benefit of torturing her mother."

Ruthie bounced and giggled at the idea..

POSTSCRIPT:

Jessica and Ruthie remain in my thoughts. With an early pregnancy, street drugs, and sexual abuse, Jessica's upbringing was bereft of more than most. There's something about Jessica prevailing—despite her abusive childhood in that remote, impoverished mining town—that hatches hope within the scope of my own career and life.

I accompanied Jessica as she said hello to her childhood sadness, loneliness, and fear. Toe-to-toe with acceptance and a bit of humor and hand-in-hand with understanding, we grew her awareness and quieted her impulse to control Ruthie. With renewed courage and strength, pain melted to nourish a garden that bloomed with love. Within this garden, Ruthie would flourish.

CHAPTER TEN

A Border Collie & Afghan Hound in Family Therapy

SHANNON AND LEXI are parents to Jacob, age eleven, and Elsa, age eight. Trouble was clearly brewing with Jacob, who had a difficult infancy and as a toddler with trouble adjusting to Elsa's arrival. Shannon spoke with rapid intensity, describing multiple ear infections, difficulty soothing him, and his insistence on sleeping with his mothers, even now as a fifth grader. They had many concerns about Jacob's struggles both at home and at school, where he had a tendency to complain and blame, back-talk teachers, and refuse to complete homework.

Lexi sat quietly on the couch showing support by occasionally interjecting pertinent examples for various scenarios.

When asked about what was going well, they described a clever and expressive child who liked to cuddle, willingly apologized for being naughty, and had a small but loyal group of close friends.

As we wrapped up our first session, I sent Shannon and Lexi home with a Family Stress Test and Parenting Tip Cards describing the four parenting styles, suggesting they have their kids vote on which "breed" they might be.

STAGE ONE: AWARENESS

Lexi and Shannon returned the next week with a Family Stress Test score of 13, putting them in the Yellow Zone. The test uncovered frequent arguing between parents, with Shannon using a frustrated or angry voice while parenting. Jacob was often angry and refused to cooperate with reasonable requests. His interactions with his sister verged on cruelty. Lexi acknowledged being distant and resentful over the many hard feelings circulating within the family. She avoids conflict and family turmoil along with Elsa, whom she refers to as the "easy child."

When asked which parenting styles they identified, Shannon spoke first, sporting a proud grin, "I got a unanimous vote for BORDER COLLIE!"

THE BORDER COLLIE

AT THEIR BEST, this parent attends to family life with vigilance and diligence and is unflagging while resolving problems.

AT THEIR WORST, this parent tends to micromanage and engage in power struggles and has fears of catastrophic outcomes

DOMINANT BELIEF: if I don't do it…it won't get done.

LOVES to be involved and assist others when help is needed.

CO-PARENTING typically chooses a companion more relaxed about the daily details of family life: the AFGHAN HOUND or GERMAN SHEPHERD.

With perked ears, busily directing and herding children, this parenting style's dog tag reads: ATTENTIVE !

"My family informed me I'm an AFGHAN HOUND," reported Lexi, admitting to being easygoing about rules due to her discomfort with arguments and conflict.

THE AFGHAN HOUND

AT THEIR BEST, this parent is pleasant and engaging and blends spontaneity with playfulness to manage tasks.

AT THEIR WORST, this parent is inconsistent and reluctant regarding rules and expectations, avoids conflict while being superficially present, and can be sullen and self-absorbed

DOMINANT BELIEFS: over time, most problems sort themselves out; children learn from their own mistakes.

LOVES TO: enjoy life and learn as you go.

CO-PARENTING: sniffs out the attentive BORDER COLLIE or compassionate GOLDEN RETRIEVER as romantic partners.

Enthralled by novelty and relishing the spontaneous over the regimented, this parenting style's dog tag reads: EASYGOING !

As is typically the case, opposites attract across the Nurture Scale, and Lexi and Shannon were no exception. When **BORDER COLLIE** and **AFGHAN HOUND** parents operate in the Yellow or Red Zones, they morph into a "GOOD COP/BAD COP" couple.

Lexi pointed at Shannon, saying, "Baaaad cop, very bad cop!"

Shannon grinned and jabbed a playful finger back at Lexi, "Good Cop! Good for *nothing* cop!"

The playfulness about their differences revealed a wonderful sense of mutual acceptance and goodwill, which indicated a relative absence of resentment. It meant we could move quickly to help Jacob.

Shannon finished the story by stating how quickly things turned into turmoil that evening. By mentioning the curse word "homework," Elsa vanished to her room, Lexi escaped to clean the kitchen, and Shannon coaxed and nagged Jacob to complete assignments.

Things got done but with the added burden of heated emotions and back talk, and a dispiriting sense of isolation in each family member.

In short, Shannon's well-intentioned intensity to motivate Jacob created a Frustration/Resistance Cycle between them. Lexi under-functioned with blithe avoidance, preferring to retreat to less emotionally demanding roles in the family.

As for Jacob, his early history of ear infections suggested chronic discomfort and left him with poor *frustration tolerance,* causing intense demands for attention and relief. When Elsa was born, Jacob subconsciously experienced a withdrawal of maternal care as parental attention was, naturally now, divided. Jacob was experiencing *attachment anxiety* that typically results in over-developed defense strategies such as blaming, complaining, and refusing; precisely the behaviors Jacob was demonstrating.

Understanding this assessment of family dynamics, Lexi and Shannon were well into the Awareness Stage on The Path to Harmony. Our clinical sessions progressed quickly.

Emotional tensions between Lexi and Shannon readily dissolved with clarification, apology, and humor. Feelings of sadness and worry were openly discussed and transformed into understanding and motivation toward change.

Soon, we were ready to for Stage Two: QUIETING.

Leaning forward, I directed my first question to Lexi—the easygoing Afghan Hound—asking what she would like to do to help the family quiet (calming conflict and anger). After a few minutes of discussion, she volunteered to offload the homework battle from Shannon and take it on herself. With cheerful agreement, I shuffled through a stack of Parenting Tip Cards and handed her Homework Best Practices.

Best Homework Practices

- Establish a consistent place and time for homework (kitchen or dining table, NOT bedroom)
- No TV or non-homework distractions allowed -- this includes adults
- Be cheerfully available for questions, but NOT hovering
- The child is invited – not commanded – to do their homework
- Bonus points: provide a light healthy snack for the child
- Allow child to face school consequences for incomplete work and remain kindly empathetic that such a thing happened. Most children will become more self-responsible within a week.

Lexi quickly scanned the card, lifted her head with a smile, and asked, "Is this all I have to do? Be cheerful and have snacks at the table while I read a book? Heck, I can do that!"

Research reveals *why* children choose to learn and complete homework: wanting to fit in with peers, teacher approval, school-based consequences, and a sense of achievement. Parental approval is surprisingly minor compared to the leverage of other accumulated influences. When parents overvalue their influence, making it about themselves, it quickly becomes counterproductive.

In the home, a caregiver's best approach to schoolwork is to provide a routine place and time where a parent cheerfully makes themselves available and social media use is curbed. In short, a parent's job is to create a comfortable and supportive environment for a child to complete their homework *should they decide to do so*.

To be clear, the main motivation for a child to do his homework lies within the child's heart: the wish to not appear different or lag behind, acceptance within social groups, and an emergent sense of the future. These subtle yet compelling motivations are quickly squashed by parental coercion in the form of constant nagging, frustration, and anger.

Understanding that homework completion is accomplished primarily due to a child's internal motivators, and not rewards or punishments doled out by caregivers, allows for the Quieting needed to dial back the Frustration/Resistance Cycle and ultimately gain a child's trust and cooperation.

It pays to remember the more frustration caregivers show, the more resistance they will get. If needed, review the Parenting Tip Card, *The Frustration/Resistance Cycle*, which describes how parental frustration brews resentment and distracts the child from more potent developmental influences.

Shannon was given permission to stand down and experiment with disengaging from arguments, nagging, and lecturing—a big ask for **BORDER COLLIES** who tend to externalize frustration by trying to manage others.

STAGE TWO: QUIETING—CREATING CALM BY MANAGING YOUR EMOTIONS

Two weeks later, Lexi and Shannon returned. Both were smiling, and before they were even seated, Lexi blurted out, "Guess who's the homework helper in the house now?" She flashed two thumbs up, "This chick!"

Lexi explained how she implemented the Homework Best Practices parenting tip card by sitting at the table with some snacks and waiting for Jacob to come around. It took a couple days, but he eventually hovered around the table. He warned her he wasn't going to do homework. She said that was fine, then invited him to play his favorite game of Straight Four. As they played, they also jabbered about things in general, and as Lexi explained, "We kinda just goofed off." Within a couple days, Jacob said, "Well, I better do my homework, or I won't get Friday Free Gym." Jacob took a seat at the table and Lexi wisely remained neutral, saying, "Sure… up to you."

It was reassuring to hear such speedy progress. Yet this buoyancy signaled I had better let Lexi and Shannon know what to expect next. In the realm of human change, few things are more inevitable than success followed by setbacks. Within the field of addiction recovery, this predictable setback is called a *relapse;* an anticipated and accepted phenomenon. The field of statistics calls this *regression to the mean.*

In the parenting domain, as support and skills are implemented, success bounces upward in incremental steps. Sooner or later, due to stress or distraction, old habits of resistance will resurface, and caregivers will experience what feels like defeat or failure. Take heart; it is merely a temporary setback. A deeper truth remains: new skills were learned and implemented, and the level of functioning was elevated.

With awareness, new skills, and mutual accord, Shannon and Lexi began to feel more at ease and stable. And Jacob, although often testy, was progressing with homework.

STAGE THREE: AWAKENING EMPATHIC ENGAGEMENT WITH CHILDREN

After a few weeks off from family therapy over spring break, Shannon and Lexi came in and settled in on the couch. Shannon announced, "You won't believe this. There must be something wrong with us, because now guess who we want to talk about?"

As a family therapist with many years of experience, this was an expected question and concern.

I smiled inwardly, knowing this new development was a positive sign for the entire family. During the last few months, as the family quieted and stabilized, a subconscious relief came over Elsa, the "easy child." She no longer needed to suppress her upset feelings (inherent to a preteen's life) so as to not rock the family boat further during turbulent times.

Now as the storm quieted, she began expressing very normal, pent-up complaints about Jacob getting all the attention. Often, these expressions had the tone and intensity Jacob showed during his turbulent times. Although alarming (especially to Shannon, who, as a BORDER COLLIE fears catastrophic outcomes), Elsa's expressions were the result of an improved family environment. She was beginning to naturally express feelings that otherwise churned in the shadowlands.

With this kind of progress, it was time to introduce skills and strategies for the third stage of the Path to Harmony: Awakening. Awakening will give Elsa and Jacob a deeper connection with their mothers, allowing upset feelings to be processed more completely within the family nest.

As emphasized throughout this book, *A child processes emotions by sharing thoughts and feelings with a trusted, attentive, and kind listener.* If the content of the child's situation exceeds the caregiver's capacity to remain calm or comprehend or amend, it's not a sign of failing. It's a sign that professional help may be needed.

> *A professional therapist provides a safe zone where openness and honesty are encouraged, dialog is mediated, and where complex emotions that exceed understanding can be processed.*

A powerful parenting strategy for Awakening is: Dosing with Love. This strategy delivers regular doses of acceptance and connection to a child. Each dose should contain an emotional tone of kindness and even adoration of the child. Like good medicine, Dosing offers relief from the Frustration/Resistance cycle that spins all too often within unstable families. Children in families operating in the Yellow and Red Zones have developed a deep ache for parental love. Dosing with Love is the antidote.

The child's ache for his parent is analogous to being thirsty but without the ability to identify or satisfy that yearning. Imagine the child as a backcountry hiker making way along a mountainous trail. A thirst distracts and degrades the hiker's stamina, decision-making, and frustration tolerance and may tempt the hiker to drink from impure puddles and ponds.

Dosing with Love is the psycho-emotional equivalent of handing a parched hiker a glass of cool, clear water. It satisfies, provides relief, and creates an emerging sense of appreciation and cooperation toward the source, especially if the water is offered on a predictable and consistent basis. Under these conditions, the hiker and person relieving thirst form a partnership of mutual reciprocation down the road.

I handed the Dosing with Love card to Shannon and Lexi.

> *DOSING WITH LOVE: Each dose, or intentional connection with a child, should contain an emotional tone of kindness and even adoration for the child.*

Dosing with LOVE!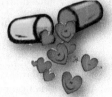

- *Need not take a lot of time (often only 20 to 30 minutes) week.*

- *Choose an enjoyable activity or game such as checkers (no electronics).*

- *If it's a competitive game, allow the child to win or even make up rules.*

- *Important to DOSE on a planned and regular basis.*

- *Expect small positive changes in the child's attitude and cooperation within 2 weeks.*

Looking up from the card, Lexi interjected, "Hey, I already do this. We have one-on-one time when I bring Elsa grocery shopping with me on Saturdays."

Lexi described how they have some really great talks in the car, but how it usually turns into a giant power struggle over something Elsa wants. The ride home and the rest of the day, unfortunately, is pretty much ruined.

I agree that bringing Elsa grocery shopping is important, but Dosing with Love has defining characteristics that make it therapeutic. Simply put, grocery trips are different than a playdate where the parent's acceptance and adoration are conveyed.

Dosing, as a therapeutic influence:

    1. Caters to the child

    2. Does not require transitions

    3. Is without distractions for the parent's attention

    4. Excludes added pressures (such as needing to behave a certain way)

Lexi quickly came up with a better plan. Elsa really enjoys puzzles. To make it special, they could make some popcorn.

I asked Lexi if she could commit to a specific day and time each week to do this activity with Elsa. Lexi chose Friday evenings, which she may have intuitively realized would make Saturday's shopping experience better.

*Over time and with practice,
Dosing With Love skills generate
spontaneous cooperation and
happiness within children.*

Shannon was curious as to her role in this Awakening part of the journey, stating she wanted to remain relevant as a parent. I chuckled, agreeing that **BORDER COLLIES** like to be ahead of the pack, and pulled one more card out of the stack for her.

I reminded Shannon how the attentive **BORDER COLLIE** parent tends to guide, critique, and advise... too much. The strategies on these Parent Tip Cards would help her become a more powerful influence on Elsa and Jacob while reducing their resistance.

Shannon read the cards, shaking her head doubtfully, but agreed to try. She suggested practicing Empathetic Listening skills on the days she drives Elsa to school. On those mornings, she agreed to use empathy statements when responding to any of Elsa's big emotions using statements beginning with, "I'm so sorry..." and, "I'm so proud...."

Responding to *INTENSE* Emotions

Allow child to FEEL

Allow child to have their version of events (don't argue!)

Do *not* give consequences or advice at this time.

> REPEAT THE PHRASE: "I'm so proud ..."
>
> "I'm so sorry ..."

EXAMPLE

Parent: "I'm so sorry you were so angry at you brother.

Child: "He's mean, and teases me about my braces.

Parent: "I'm proud you didn't hit him or hurt him.

Child: "I could have hurt if I really wanted to. Am I going to get consequences?

Parent: "We'll worry about that later. I'm just proud to have a kiddo who has the courage to talk things out.

Soon, with a can-do thumbs up, she grinned and pointed at Lexi, saying she'd do whatever was needed to stay ahead of the competition. They chuckled and walked out the door as I wished them luck.

TWO WEEKS LATER:

Lexi and Shannon came into the room about to land their signature spots on the couch, but this time Lexi plopped on Shannon's side.

Shannon stared with an open mouth, "What the hell are you doing? That's my place!"

Lexi grinned broadly, "No, ma'am, there's a new top dog in town... and it's me!"

The two moms didn't know it, but they were displaying "mood brightening," a descriptor denoting a shift away from a negative affect and toward happiness. Within families, indicators of *brightening* appear in forms like playfulness and humor. Acts of joy begin to dazzle in the emotional landscape. Caregivers report that kids play more creatively, spontaneously whistle and sing, initiate humor and silliness, and assist their siblings unasked.

These are signs of *second-order change*, meaning things are moving forward without intentional effort, and trust and kindness reciprocate between family members on a subconscious level. This is a great place to be on the Path to Harmony.

As the session moved along, the moms relived a few vignettes. Shannon had begun to hear more about the complexities of Elsa's friendships because she responded with empathy to her daughter's strong emotions. Elsa, in turn, confided to Shannon that she still missed Grandpa, how she had tried marijuana a couple times with her friends, and that a group of boys were asking for photos of her naked. Both parents had become emotionally engaged with their kids, shared in their tears, which left everyone relieved and ultimately happier afterward.

Awakening and Dosing With Love earned Elsa's trust. Curbing their instinct to lecture, warn, and advise Elsa, the parents listened with love and empathy and Elsa responded by speaking candidly and asking their advice. Elsa's moms were becoming a skilled team in helping Elsa process her emotions, which is a form of bonding and intimacy. Elsa was maturing before their very eyes.

The salve of awakening strategies like Dosing with Love and Empathic Listening skills helped Jacob also. Though still struggling with homework completion, he happily jabbered about his friends, hobbies, and interests. In time, a reading disability was detected, and the school's modifications helped ease his stress almost immediately. The good humor and acceptance surrounding him at home made school interventions tolerable rather than a negative stigma.

CHAPTER ELEVEN

German Shepherd & Golden Retriever Parents in Family Therapy

MEET LAYTON, a married thirty-nine-year-old father of Will, age eleven; Maisie, age seven. Layton came in for counseling after his wife, Janelle, threatened divorce. Managing a diesel engine repair shop, Layton works long hours. He admitted coming home tired and frustrated a lot of the time and often gets short-tempered with the kids.

Janelle had put him in the doghouse, being polite with him at best. Layton lamented there was very little warmth or affection left in their marriage. And to make matters worse, their children avoid him because of his high expectations and demands. The hope of a happy, cozy family had all but dried up. Beneath it all, he felt lonely within his own family. "The only thing I can imagine that would be lonelier," he confessed, "is waking up in an empty house."

STAGE ONE: AWARENESS: GENERATING UNDERSTANDING, ACCEPTANCE, AND STRATEGIC THINKING

In our first couple sessions we worked on awareness. Layton completed the Family Stress Test, and we discussed the specifics of his situation. Layton quickly identified himself as a **GERMAN SHEPHERD** with family stress indicators putting the family in the elevated Yellow Zone. Their stress indicators included sibling rivalry and issues with Maisy getting ready for school in the morning. His wife Janelle was most likely a **GOLDEN RETRIEVER**, which made them a classic Command and Rescue couple when stressed.

STAGE TWO: QUIETING: CREATING CALM IN THE FAMILY

When Layton understood parenting style differences could affect outcomes, it was time for a therapeutic game plan. "We have a pretty good picture of how you and your family work," I began. "What do you think we should we do next?"

Based on the information he learned about his parenting style and the stress zones, Layton could see what needed to happen. He explained, "It's pretty clear. I have to stop being the tough guy. I grew up being yelled at, and I hated it, but now that's what I'm doing with my kids." It's a bad pattern, he admitted, and he always felt horrible afterward for yelling. "I'll try to stop yelling…maybe bring all my pent up anger to you," he smirked. "At least you get paid for that kind of thing."

I assured Layton he could bring in as much anger as he needed to into my office. Along the way I would teach him new skills for handling his anger. In the meantime, I gave him the Anger Curve tip card.

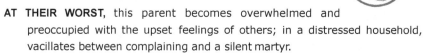

THE GOLDEN RETRIEVER

AT THEIR BEST, this parent patiently and compassionately provides emotional warmth and kindness to others and gracefully guides and cajoles children through daily routines and responsibilities.

AT THEIR WORST, this parent becomes overwhelmed and preoccupied with the upset feelings of others; in a distressed household, vacillates between complaining and a silent martyr.

DOMINANT BELIEFS: Love will conquer all. Be nice to others, and they will be nice in return.

LOVES to love and be loved.

CO-PARENTING: sniffs out principled GERMAN SHEPHERDS or easygoing AFGHAN HOUNDS.

THE GENTLE GOLDEN RETRIEVER parent style nurtures the hearts and minds of children, but the heart comes first. Therefore their dog tag reads: COMPASSIONATE !

A couple weeks later, Layton reported that he'd stopped yelling as much: "I blow it now and then, but I'm managing better. It helped to have a visual aid to realize how counterproductive yelling is."

The kids commented on the Anger Curve tip card stuck on the refrigerator and said, "Hey, Dad, that's you…the guy with the smoke coming outta his ears!"

Often the **GERMAN SHEPHERD** parent type who begins quieting (or refraining from using anger as a method of control) feels powerless and vulnerable and, frankly, doesn't like it. They feel declawed and muzzled, and it simply doesn't feel right. In the quieting stage, the **GERMAN SHEPHERD** type must learn to think and feel beyond their controlling tendencies.

As a general rule within families, beneath anger lies The Big Three Vulnerable Emotions of sadness, loneliness, and fear.

Given more empathy and compassion, children will shape themselves toward the parent's core perspectives and values.

What Layton and many parents don't realize is that children will begin to cooperate as a trailing indicator to the parent quieting. If a parent is consistent with quieting, signs of positive change in kids typically occurs within two to three weeks. The **GERMAN SHEPHERD** caregiver typically believes this approach won't work due to their dedicated belief that consequences and enforcement keep order. What Layton hadn't discovered yet is by calming himself, the kids will also feel calmer and more willing to cooperate with their father whom they admire on a primal level.

Layton was doing well, but I urged him to continue to build on his success. "Apologize to your family for yelling too much. Let them know you are working on this because you now realize it upsets them and their mom. Tell them you'll ask them, about once a week, for feedback as to how you are doing."

STAGE THREE: AWAKENING: USING EMPATHIC ENGAGEMENT WITH CHILDREN

At our next visit, Layton settled comfortably into the sofa and leaned in, "Something is *definitely* working. The kids seem more relaxed, and my wife says she sees me trying."

Layton seemed surprised that he had become more aware of when he was about to lose his cool. He leaned in even further and said he and his wife had sex for the first time in quite a while. "And it was pretty good sex. You know, *kitchen table* sex!"

Layton was making progress. He was learning to decrease his expressed

THE GERMAN SHEPHERD

AT THEIR BEST, this parent is principled and loyal to ideas and causes, rules and responsible behavior. They exude calm and stability to family life.

AT THEIR WORST, this parent becomes commanding, impatient, or angry; isolates from others with a self-righteous attitude which can appear dismissive to others; and is prone to feeling lonely.

DOMINANT BELIEFS: there are consequences, both positive and negative, to behavior, and children must learn from those consequences. Work comes before play.

LOVES to live by and instill virtues that promote responsibility and achievement.

CO-PARTNERING: chooses partners more emotionally attentive than themselves: GOLDEN RETRIEVERS and BORDER COLLIES.

The GERMAN SHEPHERD parent instills virtues and good character in children. For these reasons, this breed's dog tag reads : PRINCIPLED !

---

frustration and stop nagging and barking at the kids. His wife—feeling gratitude and relief over his emerging awareness and softer tone—was more interested in intimacy. I encouraged him to hold steady on the tiller and to course-correct whenever he slipped up.

Today, Layton was ready to learn about the next stage: Awakening.

When in the presence of a consistently calm and emotionally stable adult, children feel safe in sharing their concerns of the heart, gain relief, and ultimately become more cheerful and cooperative.

"Watch for signs of *brightening*. After being emotionally available for two or three weeks, you'll notice they'll become cheerful and playful," I explained.

Layton's eyebrows raised in curiosity.

Brightening looks like spontaneous displays of joyfulness in the form of whistling, humming, singing, silliness, or simply wanting to be helpful.

Doubt flashed across Layton's' face. It sounded too good to be true for someone who had very little hope going into therapy. "Sounds a bit like a Disney movie, but whatever. I'll try it. Let's keep this rig rolling."

With a thumbs up, I assured him that quietly listening to his children's sadness, loneliness, and fear was something he could easily do.

"What I'd like you to do until we meet again is to increase your level of nurturing, or your *emotional availability,* to the kids."

GERMAN SHEPHERDS are most comfortable doing this in the form of an activity. Layton suggested taking the kids to the big hardware store in town, where he needed some supplies to fix the deck. Both GERMAN SHEPHERD and BORDER COLLIE parents lean heavily toward educational engagement and often make the mistake of choosing an activity that is less about what their kids would be interested in and more about errands and chores that needed to get done.

I nudged Layton in a more therapeutic direction, "Here's what I recommend: think about something Will and Maisie would like to do. Choose a fun and simple activity like a board game or shooting baskets." Anything, I told him, that would promote some lighthearted banter between him and the kids. I stressed to him it should not involve electronic devices and gave him the parenting tip card, "Dosing with Love."

Dosing with LOVE!

- *Need not take a lot of time (often only 20 to 30 minutes) week.*

- *Choose an enjoyable activity or game such as checkers (no electronics).*

- *If it's a competitive game, allow the child to win or even make up rules.*

- *Important to DOSE on a planned and regular basis.*

- *Expect small positive changes in the child's attitude and cooperation within 2 weeks.*

As our time was up Layton decided he would try playing catch in the backyard, or if it was raining, a game of checkers. "We used to do that when they were younger," he stated, "I'll try that."

TWO WEEKS LATER:

Layton arrived looking more upset than happy.

"How'd the Dosing with Love experiment go?" I asked.

Layton slumped into the sofa and looked out the window, "I tried. But now they won't play with me anymore, and I'm waiting to get served divorce papers."

"*Ahhh*, let me guess," I began. "When you were playing catch, were you also trying to instruct them? Or were you winning at checkers to encourage them to be more competitive?"

He admitted that's almost exactly what happened.

I reassured Layton this was an easy fix, "Apologize to Will and Maisie for making their time with you unpleasant." I began. "Then ask them to please give you another chance and promise you'll make it fun."

Layton needs to let the kids throw the ball however they want without instruction or critique. And Layton also needed to know not to throw his fastball, or win every game of checkers. "Let them win. It's okay, even if they intentionally cheat or makeup rules. It's your job to marvel that such nice kids want to spend time with a dad who's been too bossy for too long. Got it?"

"Got it." Layton was not entirely convinced, however. "That's cool, but do we do this even if Maisie hasn't done her homework... or if Will's been fighting with his sister?"

Layton had a common concern: that his kids would be rewarded for bad behavior. Or he would be spoiling them. The answer is a resounding No! Parents do not spoil children by being kind; to the contrary, their influence on them grows.

Children will complete and learn from homework due to:

A. their interest in the topic

B. to gain parent and teacher approval

C. to follow norms and behaviors of classroom peer group

D. to establish and maintain a certain standing within their peer group

E. concern about school-based consequences

F. their emerging realization of the future and maturation.

I leaned in and looked Layton in the eye. It was important he heard this, "By being patient and kind to your children, you are helping them feel loved; and when they feel loved, they will want to emulate you."

Layton's eyebrows raised, and I continued, "You'll notice they'll become more cooperative and more likely to do the things you were trying to get them to do when commanding and critiquing." Then handed him the Frustration/Resistance Parenting Tip Card.

After a few weeks, Layton reported things had greatly improved. Will and Maisy each got a day after school to play a board game with their father. Not only had Will began to laugh and goof around more, but he also talked more openly about the worries and concerns of his young heart. Will was visibly happier. Layton grinned broadly, "He enters a room whistling and is even starting to help around the house!"

Layton also noticed an improvement in his relationship with Maisy, who was doing homework with less fuss.

Finally, Layton began using the strategy I call, "lead and they will follow." Rather than barking out orders at bedtime, he began yawning and stretching. Then, he would invite Maisy upstairs to brush teeth with him and read a story. Maisy resisted a few times, but Layton sat patiently in the reading chair with a book in his hand talking out loud to himself (and to any little girl who might be listening), about how sad he felt alone without his smart and helpful daughter.

The family was shifting away from the edge of the Red Zone and toward the more rewarding Green Zone.

POSTSCRIPT: ACCIDENTAL MOVE TOWARD LOVE.

As things bumbled along (bumbling is the only way love moves), Layton asked his wife to join him for a session. They sat close but not touching each other on the couch.

"Thanks for coming in today, Janelle," I started, "It's been quite a journey, hasn't it?"

Yes, she agreed, it had. Then her head tipped down, and tears fell from her eyes. Layton looked confused.

I glanced down at her, hands tightly folded in her lap. Layton caught my cue and held her hand.

Janelle sniffed, "Oh Layton, you're such an ass." Looking into each other's eyes, they both chuckled and shed some tears.

I smiled, "Janelle, you're right. Sometimes, Layton is an ass, and Janelle...

he's determined to work harder to be a better man so the kids don't fear him, and so someday he might have access to your heart again."

What Janelle might not realize: the GERMAN SHEPHERD *parent, with shield and spear on the outside, has a marshmallow center, aching for the love and kindness she carries in her heart.*

Janelle and Layton returned in the following months to peek into the shadows of their marriage. Discovering shared sorrow generates relief—which is the better part of love— and emotional closeness soon followed….

CHAPTER TWELVE

Afghan Hound & Border Collie in Family Therapy

TOGETHER ABOUT FIFTEEN YEARS, Jake and Vikki were parents to three children: a fifteen-year-old, a thirteen-year-old, and a ten-year-old.

Vikki arrived at our first session announcing that Jake would be a little late because, she said with a forced smile, "That's just the way he rolls. I want to get things going, Mr. Buckley." She continued, "We took your tests. I'm a BORDER COLLIE, he's an AFGHAN HOUND, and we scored 17 on the Family Stress Test."

Their family's Stress Test score of 17 put them in the Red Zone. AFGHAN HOUND and BORDER COLLIE co-parents in the Red Zone meant they were parenting as a Good Cop/ Bad Cop couple.

As I've learned to expect from a BC, Vikki wanted to get the ball rolling quickly. "I wanted to make this appointment three months ago, but it was March Madness, and he had his brackets to worry about. Then he wanted to wait because he thought things were getting better. Only now, because I threatened divorce, is he willing to come see you."

Vikki described her husband as extremely charming and likable. "Everyone loves him," she said with dramatic flair. "He's easygoing and smooth-talking. He'll want you to believe our family problems are minor stuff, not worth getting worked up about. Actually, he'll probably suggest I need some therapy to help me calm down."

Jake had a way of avoiding issues and conflict, she added.

"Go ahead and take a breath, Vikki. I'm getting the picture." I interrupted for no other reason than to prevent poor Vikki from exhausting herself.

So much was going on in Vikki's life, and she was obviously overwhelmed. As she saw it, the two most important things in her life were on the line: her children's well-being and her marriage. "It sounds like you feel alone in parenting," I said.

She inhaled deeply. I continued, "You feel abandoned by his nonchalant approach to parenting, and you want more from him, is that right?"

Vikki tilted her head warily as I spoke, "I really don't need that empathy stuff. I'd rather not dwell on how tired and pissed off I am. It just makes me depressed. But yes, for the sake of our children and our marriage, I want him to get on board and parent."

This tendency to keep busy while avoiding feelings is a hallmark of BORDER COLLIE attribute and confirmed I was sniffing down the right trail.

Vikki admitted to being controlling to the point of overbearing, "But it's because I have to do everything! Jake has to step it up." She explained, "Our ten-year-old is still wetting the bed, and our thirteen-year-old refuses to get off his phone. If Jake doesn't get on the *same page* with parenting, I'm done with this marriage!"

As if on cue, there was a soft rap on the door. A tall, lanky man peeked in. I waved Jake in, and he slid into the room with a slow, graceful gait. Silently he assessed his wife's frustration-flushed face, lowered himself into a chair, and said with a pained smile, "Hey, I see she's filled you in."

Sensing how polarized Vikki and Jake were as a BORDER COLLIE and AFGHAN HOUND couple in the Red Zone, I suggested we allow Vikki to get on with her day so Jake and I could take some initiative around some of her concerns.

I'm sure this wasn't what Vikki was expecting, but it was clear where to start. Rising from the sofa, she turned to her husband and poked a finger at him, "The washer repair guy comes at eleven. You'll need to be home to let him in!"

Jake and I watched her stride swiftly out of the office. He unfolded a piece of paper, "These are the things I'm supposed to work on," he said, passing the paper to me.

"Why argue with a force of nature?" I grinned.

Jake shrugged and added, "Or a freight train."

I suggested we settle on "BORDER COLLIE," knowing he and Vikki had already figured out their parenting styles. "Why don't you tell me your thoughts about what's going on in your family?"

Home life, in Jake's view, was a three-ring circus of chaos, conflict, and way too many structured activities. Homework completion was a growing problem, mostly according to Vikki, who blamed him for his lack of participation. Screen time was also a constant battle between parents and kids. He and Vikki weren't able to agree on rules surrounding either screen time or homework.

"The two youngest are becoming increasingly absorbed with online gaming," he lamented. "I'm tired of telling them to shut it off only to be bombarded with never-ending tantrums."

Much to Vikki's dismay, Jake ends up appeasing the kids with extended play time simply to stop the howling. Morning routines are equally painful as Vikki tries to get kids out the door. Vikki and Jake have yet to become a united front.

STAGE ONE: AWARENESS: GENERATING UNDERSTANDING, ACCEPTANCE, AND STRATEGIC THINKING

Learning his parenting style, Jake understood he was on the *FLEXIBLE* end of the Structure Scale and the ENCOURAGE end of the Nurture Scale. Vikki, I explained, was on the *FIRM* end of the Structure Scale, and the COMFORT end of the Nurture Scale. Jake could picture how these parenting style differences could lead to conflict between the two of them.

I asked Jake to take the Family Stress Survey for himself. "Yeah," he admitted, "I guess we're pretty much in the Red Zone. She threw the "D" word at me without even blinking." When I described the **AFGHAN HOUND** parent style as laissez-faire, Jake gave a knowing chuckle. He looked rightly concerned, however, when I described how this parenting style can demonstrate a "shallowness of felt presence."

Shallowness of felt presence (being there, but contributing little emotional support or leadership to the family flow) can cause kids to feel insecure during times of distress and cause spouses to feel abandoned.

Jake looked down at his hands, "I work the second shift, so I've left pretty much all the family stuff to Vikki. I mean, what am I supposed to do? I blame Vikki for nagging and yelling and creating a ton of tension for everyone. But, I don't know…maybe I've bailed on her."

After surveying their family routines and how they're working, Jake and I agreed to work in the morning hours.

"Mornings are the hardest for us because it sets the tone for the whole day," said Jake. "A lot is my fault because I sleep in late. After work, I have a hard time going straight to bed and have a bad habit of staying up to watch TV, so I'm tired and grumpy in the morning. I either stay in bed till they're out the door, or I find somewhere quiet to hang out."

Fortunately, Jake was willing to accept some personal responsibility and was capable of some honest introspection.

At the end of our session, he asked where he should start.

"That's easy," I told him, "And you'll be good at it! Just put this Frustration/ Resistance Cycle parenting tip card on the refrigerator, reminding you to be like Barney the dinosaur…you know, 'I love you. You love me. We're a happy fam-i-ly.'"

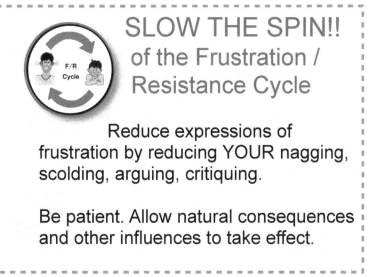

Jake laughed, "I think I can do that!" With a wave, he reiterated, "Be like Barney." And off he went, announcing over his shoulder, he would be in touch soon.

QUIETING & AWAKENING (IN THIS SCENARIO, BOTH QUIETING AND AWAKENING OCCUR IN UNISON)

Three weeks later, Jake returned with an update.

"I'm kinda surprised," he began, "a lot of things are sorta fixing themselves. First of all, I put the **AFGHAN HOUND** description card on the fridge. Eli, my oldest, told me I was totally the dog on the fridge."

THE AFGHAN HOUND

AT THEIR BEST, this parent is pleasant and engaging and blends spontaneity with playfulness to manage tasks.

AT THEIR WORST, this parent is inconsistent and reluctant regarding rules and expectations, avoids conflict while being superficially present, and can be sullen and self-absorbed.

DOMINANT BELIEFS: over time, most problems sort themselves out; children learn from their own mistakes.

LOVES TO: enjoy life and learn as you go.

CO-PARENTING: sniffs out the attentive BORDER COLLIE or compassionate GOLDEN RETRIEVER as romantic partners.

Enthralled by novelty and relishing the spontaneous over the regimented, this parenting style's dog tag reads: EASYGOING !

THE BORDER COLLIE

AT THEIR BEST, this parent attends to family life with vigilance and diligence and is unflagging while resolving problems.

AT THEIR WORST, this parent tends to micromanage and engage in power struggles and has fears of catastrophic outcomes.

DOMINANT BELIEF: if I don't do it…it won't get done!

LOVES to be involved and assist others when help is needed.

CO-PARENTING typically chooses a companion more relaxed about the daily details of family life: the AFGHAN HOUND or GERMAN SHEPHERD.

With perked ears, busily directing and herding children, this parenting style's dog tag reads:ATTENTIVE !

Jake was stunned. "Paul, my kids think I avoid them. Everything I do, I do for them, and yet they think I don't want to be with them." Jake looked away sadly, "I could barely breathe. I kept thinking about what you said about that 'shallowness of felt presence.'"

Eli's words had hit their mark. Jake decided to get up every morning to be with his kids. "No excuses, I decided. And that's what I've been doing. Nothing fancy," he marveled. "All I do is sit there with my coffee and talk with them."

"That's the ticket!" I said.

I asked him if he noticed any change in the kids.

Jake's eyes twinkled, "We laugh more. Sometimes they fight, so I tell them to settle down, or I'll kiss them in public...silly stuff. That usually does it. Sometimes, I start singing the Barney song. Homework is getting better, too. On weekends, I stopped watching CNN and just hang with them. I'm into the family more."

Jake beamed, "I'm actually happier this way, and the kids seem to like me better."
"You look happy," I told him. "You also sound proud of yourself."

I let Jake know I was proud of him too. Few people make so much progress so quickly.

SIDE NOTE: When Jake said he was being silly with his kids, it reminded me of one mom (a **BORDER COLLIE**) who decided to switch from her serious, parenting voice to using a silly robot voice or goofy accent when reminding her kid to do his chores. Much to her surprise, her son would grin and giggle and, more often than not, happily comply.

In Jake's example, the Parenting Tip Cards on the refrigerator generated talking points for a brave child willing to share sensitive feelings with his father. These daily reminders placed a gentle leash around Jake and guided him away from his natural tendency to drift in an under-involved manner.

Jake dedicated himself to being more involved with the details of their children's lives, deliberately moving toward the Green Zone on the MAP. In the language of Attachment Theory, he *attended* and *attuned* to the daily routines of his children. In this way, the kids felt their father's nurturing and broadening support. His "felt presence" grew deeper roots within the family. In this fertile garden of compassion, hearts began to blossom.

In the weeks following, Vikki reported progress. With Jake's more active involvement, she felt some of the parenting burden lifted. But she admitted to having little affection for her husband because, as she said, "So much has gone so wrong for too long."

She told the story of how, after the C-section birth of their second child, Jake took a four-day fishing trip.

"Vikki's mom was staying for a week to help out," he argued, to convince her that he should take a break so he could return fresh and ready to help.

She continued, "There are so many things wrong with what he did, I'm not sure I'll ever be able to forget how abandoned I felt. He left me on the couch, in stitches. Holding *his* child." She looked directly into Jake's eyes, saying with resignation, "With all that's happened, I don't think I'll ever be able to forgive or trust you again."

The room was a cocoon of sorrow, and Jake reached for a tissue, wiped his eyes, and set a tissue on his wife's knee as well.

At its best, psychotherapy can be a sacred confluence of honesty, courage, authenticity, and vulnerability. This was one of those moments.

I named the obvious core of this couple's dearness and pain. "Jake, you're a blessed man to hear from your wife the unvarnished truth of her heart." And I continued, "Vikki, I'm glad in this moment your husband allowed himself to hear your hurt and pain. Today, it was measured in tears, not argument and evasion."

Jake continued with therapy, learning how to accept his children's vulnerable feelings of sadness, loneliness, and fear while also finding ways to accept Vikki's anger and resentment as a wound for which he was culpable.

Vikki's hurt and dissatisfaction fueled Jake's resolve to move his family toward the Green Zone. Mustering self-discipline, he managed the children by implementing The 3Rs (Rules, Respect, and Responsibilities). Full engagement with the children was becoming a habit.

When I asked him how he was able to change course so quickly and so well, he answered in a snap, "That's easy. I swore I'd never abandon my wife again. I'm enforcing the rules and routines she established for our family. If I'm honest with myself, I know she's put much more time and research into best parenting practices, so I'm doing what makes her happy. Happy wife, happy life." He also admitted, "I've been acting like a twelve-year-old most of my marriage."

POSTSCRIPT:

Jake and Vikki eventually separated. Vikki parented from the home nest, and Jake from a small house just down the street. They both seemed happier and began going out on dates and having fun again. She visited my office about a year later. Feeling betrayed as a child by her father's drug use decades ago, she also felt abandoned by Jake for a long time. "I am so tired of being angry at everyone, even my kids," she murmured, but this time, as her foot tapped nervously, Jake was there holding her hand.

I told her what she already knew: all those feelings are exhausting to carry around. I told her I was proud of her for carrying such a load in order to form the worthy life she was living. Now was a good time to melt the anger and befriend the hidden hurt in her life. Over the next year, she did just that.

EPILOGUE

"You're braver than you believe, stronger than you seem, and smarter than you think."
WINNIE THE POOH

OUR JOURNEY HAS COME TO AN END for the time being. Traveling through these pages, we arrived at a better place, a place of improved family dynamics.

Consider how much you have accomplished. A canine avatar accompanied you along three stages: Awareness, Quieting, and Awakening. The Family Stress Test estimated how lost in parenting confusion you were: Green, Yellow, or Red Zone. The dangers of The Frustration/ Resistance Cycle were identified as dark paths to avoid. Parenting Tip Cards sprinkled a sunnier path, guiding along the way. And finally, examples of parents in family therapy told stirring tales of their own crossings from shadowlands of frustration to a brighter destination of harmony and cooperation.

It's time to practice these concepts, strategies, and examples while forging ahead. Take small steps. Find support. Consider going to therapy to assist with overwhelming complexities and emotional blockages.

Family life is the most maddening and most meaningful endeavor in life. Continue to laugh and cry while engaging with the vulnerable feelings of children.

As Ruthie told her mother Angela, "Mom, I used to hate how much I hated you. Now I love how much I love you."

FURTHER RESOURCES

The Archaeology of Mind: Neuro-evolutionary Origins of Human Emotion. Panksepp, J., and Biven, L. (2012). New York: W. W. Norton & Company.

The Five-Factor Model of Personality. Edited by Jerry S. Wiggins (1996). New York: The Guilford Press.

Patterns of Attachment: A Psychological Study of the Strange Situation. Mary Salter Ainsworth, Mary C. Blehar, Everett Walters, and Sally N. Wall (2015). New York and London, Routledge, Taylor & Francis Group

A Secure Base: Parent-Child Attachment and Healthy Human Development. John Bowlby (1988) Basic Books of the Perseus Books Group.

Love Sense: The Revolutionary New Science of Romantic Relationships. Sue Johnson (2013), New York: Little Brown Spark

ACKNOWLEDGMENTS

*A salute to my parents, Ruth and Bill, who married
in 1950 and, in time, delivered me and my four siblings,
Bill, Becky, Greg, and Tim to the prairies and sparkled
lakes of midwestern Minnesota.
While writing these pages, in spirit and memory,
each of you has prompted and inspired me.*

*To Sharon Davis, who illustrated the book and wrangled my wondering
mind. This book would not be possible without you.*

*Jerry and Lilah, your support came at the right time, even
though my deadlines lagged. Thank you.*

*Rob Wething, Paul Kelleher, and Scott Sater thanks for your humorous
prods and feedback.*

ABOUT THE AUTHOR

Author and therapist, Paul Buckley has helped marriages and families in distress for over three decades. A lighthearted and charismatic speaker, Paul gives educational workshops to parents, educators, potential foster parents, and trains others working in family therapy.

Based in the Twin Cites of Minnesota, with a Master's in Family and Marriage therapy, Paul bases his practice on the sound footings of Attachment and Emotion Focused Theory and Panksepp's neuroscience research. His work teaches parents and educators how to be a therapeutic influence on children, transforming vulnerable emotions of sadness, fear, and loneliness into elastic bonds of shared love.

If you see him on a trout stream or cross country ski trail be sure to say hi!

For media guest appearances, or information on workshops on
Parenting Styles Unleashed: A Modern Guide to Improved Family Dynamics
contact Paul at mystrongfamily.com

Printed in the USA
CPSIA information can be obtained
at www.ICGtesting.com
LVHW010115271024
794816LV00002B/273